The Supernatural Thread *in* METHODISM

The Supernatural Thread *in* METHODISM

SIGNS *and* WONDERS AMONG METHODISTS THEN *and* NOW

DR. FRANK H. BILLMAN

CHP

THE SUPERNATURAL THREAD IN METHODISM
by Aldersgate Renewal Ministries (ARM), with Dr. Frank H. Billman
Published by Creation House Press (CHP)
A Charisma Media Company
600 Rinehart Road
Lake Mary, Florida 32746
www.charismamedia.com

Unless otherwise noted, all Scripture quotations are from the Holy Bible, New International Version®. Copyright © 1973, 1978, 1984 by International Bible Society. Used by permission of Zondervan Publishing House. All rights reserved.

Scripture quotations marked MSG are from *The Message: The Bible in Contemporary English*, copyright © 1993, 1994, 1995, 1996, 2000, 2001, 2002. Used by permission of NavPress Publishing Group.

Scripture quotations marked NLT are from the Holy Bible, New Living Translation, copyright © 1996, 2004, 2007. Used by permission of Tyndale House Publishers, Inc., Wheaton, IL 60189. All rights reserved.

Scripture quotations marked NKJV are from the New King James Version of the Bible. Copyright © 1979, 1980, 1982 by Thomas Nelson, Inc., publishers. Used by permission.

Scripture quotations marked ESV are from the Holy Bible, English Standard Version. Copyright © 2001 by Crossway Bibles, a division of Good News Publishers. Used by permission.

Design Director: Bill Johnson
Cover design by Terry Clifton

Visit the Aldersgate website: www.aldersgaterenewal.org

Library of Congress Cataloging-in-Publication Data: 2013941267
International Standard Book Number: 978-1-62136-406-1
E-book International Standard Book Number: 978-1-62136-407-8

Permission has been requested for some sources quoted and cited by the author.

While the author has made every effort to provide accurate telephone numbers and Internet addresses at the time of publication, neither the publisher nor the author assumes any responsibility for errors or for changes that occur after publication.

13 14 15 16 17 — 9 8 7 6 5 4 3
Printed in the United States of America

TABLE OF CONTENTS

TABLE OF CONTENTS

FOREWORD

EUGENE PETERSON PARAPHRASED the prayer of Habakkuk, saying, "God, I've heard what our ancestors say about you, and I'm stopped in my tracks, down on my knees. Do among us what you did among them. Work among us as you worked among them. And as you bring judgment, as you surely must, remember mercy" (3:1–2, MSG). When I reflect on the spiritual journey of Rev. Dr. Frank Billman on the path to writing *The Supernatural Thread in Methodism*, those very words come to mind. Posturing his heart as a student in diligent pursuit of understanding our Methodist heritage, Frank has genuinely been stopped in his tracks and is down on his knees in intercession for God to "do among us what [He] did among them." His unquenchable pursuit for the "more" of God has resulted in a resource that I believe will prompt that very prayer in us: "Work among us as You worked among them."

Along the journey, Frank has exemplified the longing that Paul expressed to the Galatians: "Oh, my dear children! I feel as if I'm going through labor pains for you again, and they will continue until Christ is fully developed in your lives" (4:19, NLT). Frank's example of humility, authenticity, accessibility, and integrity has been a winsome witness of the Spirit's ability to develop both the character and the power of Christ in a life. While the knowledge he has gained through his relentless research could have easily "puffed him up," Frank has exemplified edifying love and offered a gift to the body of Christ.

In Psalm 78, as the history of Israel is chronicled, a painful indictment is found in verse 11: They "forgot His works and His wonders that He had shown them" (NKJV). For readers of *The Supernatural Thread in Methodism*, this indictment is countered; faith that God is able and willing to use ordinary people to accomplish His extraordinary purposes is ignited; and courage to step out and trust God in ministry is imparted. I am just one of many who can testify to that with a hearty "Amen!"

—JONATHAN DOW,
EXECUTIVE DIRECTOR, ALDERSGATE RENEWAL MINISTRIES

PREFACE

THE PROPHET AMOS told king Amaziah, "I was neither a prophet, nor a prophet's son, but I was a shepherd, and I also took care of sycamore-fig trees. But the Lord took me from tending the flock and said, 'Go prophesy to my people Israel'" (Amos 7:14–15).

I am not a church historian, nor the son of a church historian. I am a shepherd of a flock of United Methodists and have been such a shepherd since 1979. As an elder in the United Methodist Church, I took the course in Methodist history required by the *Discipline* at one of our official United Methodist seminaries. I enjoyed the course, because I have always had an interest in history.

Long after the seminary course was over, as a United Methodist pastor, I began to read more works about Methodist history that would include stories about the power of God being manifested among the Methodists. I would read articles that also told about incidents where the power of God "showed up" among the Methodists. And I became aware of contemporary stories of the Spirit of God moving in power among Methodists in the United States and around the world. I also personally observed that power moving among Methodists. I wondered why I had never learned about these things in our United Methodist seminary.

I began to collect the stories and share the stories. I shared them at Aldersgate Conferences, at the Methodist School for Supernatural Ministry, and in other settings. Many United Methodists were as surprised as I was to learn of a whole part of their heritage that no one had ever told them about. There are Methodist historians who do report these stories in their works, but I have not been aware of a book that draws these stories together to highlight this particular theme in Methodist history. And I am not aware of a book that reports on the supernatural work of God among United Methodists today.

After sharing this part of our Methodist history and God's acts among us today, a number of people would come up to me and ask, "When are you going to write this in a book?"

At one point I was in a seminar with Linda Gregorino, a dear saint connected with Aldersgate Renewal Ministries who has recently gone to be with the Lord. Linda had been given prophetic gifts and discernment. She had been called "the Bag Lady" because God often sent her into a store and had her buy various small items. She would have no idea at the time why she was buying that item. Then she would come into a ministry situation with her bag of purchases, pull one out, look at it, look at the crowd, and God would tell her the person to give it to and what to say to the person. Numerous times a person receiving such a "gift" and word from God would burst into tears, being deeply touched by God through Linda's ministry.

In one session, Linda reached into her bag and pulled out a pen. She came right up to me, gave me the pen, and said, "Write it!" At that moment I knew God was speaking to me about writing a number of books from ideas that God had been giving me. This book is one of them.

God told Amos, "Go prophesy to My people Israel." I am not so bold as to say that God has said to me, "Go prophesy to My people called United Methodists," but I do believe that there is a message here that our church needs to hear. God has moved in powerful, supernatural ways in the past. God did that in the Bible and in church history. God did it among Methodists in the past, and He continues to do that today, even among United Methodists.

I have heard people wonder if God is done with the United Methodist Church. I am certain that God is not done with us. God continues to work supernaturally among United Methodists today. I continue to hear testimonies of Methodists who left our church, whom God later sent back into our church. I also hear more and more stories of people from other denominations whom God has sent into our church. Why would God do these things if our church is coming to an end?

I hope as you read these stories, that you will be encouraged. I hope you will be encouraged to seek a greater manifestation of the supernatural power of God in your life and in the life of your church. I hope you will be hope-full, that the God who acted supernaturally among Methodists in the past would do the same for you and your church today.

—FRANK H. BILLMAN, A FELLOW SERVANT

INTRODUCTION

I F YOU WERE to think of Methodism as a garment, there would
be many threads that make up that garment. One would be John
Wesley's emphasis on grace. Another would be his social concern
for the poor, widows, and those in prison. Still another would be his
emphasis on organization and accountability, as seen in the class
meetings and annual conference structure.

Some threads in a garment are more important than others. If some
of the lesser important threads are removed, the garment may have a
run or a pull and the garment would be marred but still useable. On
the other hand, if important threads are removed, a whole sleeve or
leg may fall off of the garment. It would no longer be recognizable as
the original garment.

I believe that one of those important threads in the garment of
Methodism historically is the belief in and participation in the supernatural ministry of the Holy Spirit. Supernatural manifestations of
the power of the Holy Spirit were common, expected, and sought after
by Methodists. This is a thread in the garment of Methodism that
seems to be overlooked or ignored quite often as Methodists look at
their history.

This thread of supernatural ministry is important because it goes
back to the Bible. In the Old Testament, we see a God who supernaturally delivered the people of Israel out of slavery in Egypt and
brought them to the Promised Land. He performed miracles through
prophets like Elijah and Elisha. In the New Testament, we see that
a large part of Jesus' ministry was supernatural—healing the sick,
casting out demons, cleansing lepers, raising the dead, walking on
water, changing water into wine, multiplying loaves and fishes, and
many other miracles. Luke says in Acts 2:22 that Jesus was "a man
accredited to you by signs, wonders, and miracles." The disciples, with

Jesus and then by themselves, as recorded in the Book of Acts, also did supernatural ministry.

After Bible times, we see that God's supernatural ministry through His people continued. We shall see that "cessationists" arose, who believed that God's working supernaturally "ceased" with the completion of the Bible or with the death of the last of the apostles, but this is simply not supported by church history. Miracles and supernatural ministry continued right through church history, among the Moravians and then with John Wesley and the Methodists. It is important to understand this history—not just because it is Methodist but because it is biblical. It is one long important, powerful thread that goes all the way back to the Bible.

If a thread of one color is joined by many others of the same color, the whole garment takes on that color. So if the supernatural thread was green, many Methodists and Methodist churches were green in the past, and many outside the United States are green today.

Was every Methodist and Methodist church moving in the supernatural in the past? Of course not. Some Methodists, Methodist pastors, and Methodist churches wanted nothing to do with "enthusiasm." But like it or not, many were moving in the supernatural, and this was still a major part of their heritage.

This book will explore the supernatural heritage of Methodists around the world and highlight some of the supernatural ministry being done by United Methodists today.

Chapter One

SUPERNATURAL MANIFESTATIONS IN CHURCH HISTORY

From Biblical Times to the Wesleys

WHAT ARE SUPERNATURAL MANIFESTATIONS?

WHEN WE TALK about supernatural manifestations, what are we talking about? People say, "When I witnessed the birth of my first child, that was a miracle!" Or, "Each new day is a miracle." Some refer to a "miracle berry," "miracle drugs," or the "miracles of modern science." The term *miracle* is attached to many different experiences. The fact is, if everything is a miracle, then there are no miracles.

The *Random House Dictionary of the English Language* defines the word *miracle* as "an effect or extraordinary event in the physical world that surpasses all known human or natural powers and is ascribed to a supernatural cause." So, by definition, if something happens all the time, it is ordinary, not extraordinary, and is therefore not a miracle. And if it is caused by human effort rather than by a supernatural cause, it is not a miracle. So, a first child being born is moving and dramatic but not a miracle because babies are born every day. But if a baby is detected by doctors to have died in the womb and is then born alive, that would be a miracle. When we refer to supernatural manifestations, we mean times when God moves in our world and causes results that can be experienced by our human senses but not explained.

Of course, any work of the Holy Spirit that causes a notable change in something could be considered a manifestation of the Spirit. We are born again by the Spirit of God, so we receive a new life by the Spirit.

Our sanctification, the growth of the fruit of the Spirit in our lives, is a work of the Spirit. But for our purposes in this book, I want to focus on God suddenly moving in our world in a miraculous, supernatural way so that there is a manifestation of that movement of God in signs, wonders, miracles, and/or gifts of the Spirit.

BIBLICAL EXAMPLES OF SUPERNATURAL MANIFESTATIONS

There are abundant examples of these manifestations in the Bible. I will only mention a few. In the Old Testament, there is the pillar of cloud and fire, the parting of the sea, the manna from heaven, the provision of quail, the water from the rock, and the stopping of the waters of the Jordan so the people could cross. There were Elijah and Elisha both bringing dead people back to life, the healing of Naaman, the miraculous supply of oil for the widow, and a dead man coming back to life when his body touched the bones of Elisha in his grave. There were revivals under Josiah in 2 Kings 22–23 and under Ezra in Nehemiah 8.

Then in 2 Chronicles 5:13–14, at the dedication of Solomon's temple, we read that the house of the Lord was filled with a cloud so that the priests could not stand to minister because of the cloud. The passages about this dedication of the temple mention the cause being the *glory of God*. The Hebrew word for *glory* means "weight" or "heaviness." It was as if the presence of God was so strong and so weighty and so overpowering that the people could not stand up. This same problem is mentioned in Exodus 40:35, when Moses completes and dedicates the tabernacle. The priests being unable to stand due to the presence of the power of God could be an early example of what we call *resting in the Spirit* today, where people fall over or slump to the ground under the power of the Holy Spirit.

Jesus' ministry was, of course, filled with manifestations of the Spirit. I won't take time to enumerate them. But I would note some of the places where Jesus told His followers to do those same things. In Matthew 10:8, when Jesus sent out the twelve, He told them to heal the sick, raise the dead, cleanse lepers, and cast out demons. When He sent out the seventy in Luke 10, He told them to heal the sick and cast out demons. Then in the various times of commissioning His disciples at the end of His ministry, He told His disciples in Matthew 28:20 to teach them "to do *all* that I have commanded you." That *all* would include what he told them in Matthew 10:8—to heal the sick, raise the dead, cleanse lepers, and cast out demons. In Mark 16:17–18, Jesus says, "These signs will accompany those who believe: In my name they will drive out demons; they will speak in new tongues; they will pick up snakes with their hands; and when they drink deadly poison, it will not hurt them at all; they will place their hands on sick people, and they will get well." In John 14:11–12, Jesus says, "Believe me when I say that I am in the Father and the Father is in me; or at least believe on the evidence of the miracles themselves.... Anyone who has faith in me will do what I have been doing. He will do even greater things than these because I am going to the Father." And at the end of John's Gospel, in John 20:21, Jesus says, "As the Father has sent me, even so I am sending you." In other words, "As the Father sent me to do all these things you have seen Me do, I am sending you to do the same things." Finally, in Acts 1:8, Jesus says, "You shall receive power and you shall be my witnesses." Many sermons have been preached on this scripture about us getting the power to witness, but that is not what it says. It says, "You shall receive power and you shall be witnesses." In other words, God's power in and through you will witness; you will be a witness because people will see the manifestation of God's power in your life.

On the Day of Pentecost, we read that the Holy Spirit did come in power on the disciples and there were manifestations. We read of speaking in tongues unknown to the speakers. Some onlookers accused the disciples of being drunk. Would that accusation have come if the disciples were just sitting there, quietly praying in other languages— if that was the only manifestation going on there? Drunken people don't just babble on in unintelligible speech. They stagger and stumble, and sometimes they fall down. Sometimes they are unable to move. Sometimes they laugh a lot. Sometimes they cry. It is quite likely that some of the disciples were falling down or exhibiting other manifestations of the power of the Spirit on the Day of Pentecost in addition to speaking in tongues. Peter drew his listeners' attention to "what you now see and hear" (Acts 2:33).

If the priests at the dedication of Solomon's temple could no longer stand up to minister when the power and presence of God filled the physical temple, it would not be unexpected that people on the Day of Pentecost would fall down and display other manifestations when the presence and power of God came and filled the bodies of the disciples, the new temples. If strange things happened when the Holy Spirit came at Pentecost, should we really be surprised when strange things happen when the Holy Spirit comes again and again?

And as we read through the Book of Acts, we see that the power of the Holy Spirit was manifested in the lives of the apostles just as Jesus promised. We see healings and miracles and exorcisms and raising the dead and spiritual gifts being exercised. Paul told the Corinthians, "My message and my preaching were not with wise and persuasive words, but with a demonstration of the Spirit's power, so that your faith might not rest on men's wisdom, but on God's power" (1 Cor. 2:4). Later in that letter, he wrote, "For the kingdom of God is not a matter of talk but of power" (1 Cor. 4:20). And he wrote to the Romans, "I will not venture to speak of anything except what Christ has accomplished through me in leading the Gentiles to obey God by what I have said and done—by the power of signs and miracles, through the power of the Spirit" (Rom. 15:18–19).

What About Church History?

If we are to look at the supernatural manifestations of the Spirit among the Methodists, it is important to first take a look at the church history that led up to the Methodists.

So, what happened when the last of the apostles died? There are whole denominations, Bible schools, and seminaries teaching that with the death of the last of the apostles and the writing of the last book of the Bible, around AD 100, these manifestations of the Spirit— signs, wonders, miracles, and spiritual gifts—all ceased. This is the view reflected in John Darby's (1800–1882) *dispensationalism* and the notes of the Scofield Reference Bible. Their view is that these manifestations were part of that dispensation, that age of church history, but are not legitimately occurring today. Any supposed manifestations today are of either human or demonic origin.

The biggest problem with that view is that it is not supported by church history. As you leave the time of the New Testament and come into the period of the church fathers, these men recorded that manifestations of the Spirit continued in the life of the church. However, certain trends began to emerge that limited these manifestations. Paul had warned his readers to not quench the Spirit. Why would he have said that if that was not already happening? And during church history, we can see several things that happened to quench the Spirit. Yet even then, when people truly sought God and when they sought to be open to His Spirit, God continued to move in signs and wonders.

The Early Church

All three books of the Shepherd of Hermas are a recital of his extraordinary gifts—his visions, prophecies, and revelations.[1]

Justin Martyr, who wrote about fifty years after the apostles, says, "There are prophetic gifts among us even until now. You may see with us both women and men having gifts from the Spirit of God." And he insists that anyone could see with their own eyes Christians casting out devils.[2]

One of the many witnesses to the manifestations in the early church was Irenaeus (130–200). He wrote, "Those who are in truth His disciples, receiving grace from Him, do in His name perform miracles.... For some do certainly and truly drive out devils.... Others still, heal the sick by laying their hands upon them, and they are made whole." Irenaeus said, regarding raising the dead, that it was frequently performed on necessary occasions by great fasting and the joint supplication of the church. And he reported that "we hear many speaking with all kinds of tongues, and expounding the mysteries of God."[3]

Theophilus, bishop of Antioch, who lived in the same time as Irenaeus, speaks of casting out devils as then common in the church.[4]

Montanus led a movement named for him around AD 156. It was a charismatic reformation complete with speaking in tongues, prophecies, visions, and an expectation of the soon return of Jesus Christ. Unfortunately, it had its share of excesses and fanaticism. Because it

posed a threat to established Christianity, it was formally condemned
by the synods of Asia Minor. John Wesley considered the Montanists
true Christians rather than heretics.[5]

Francis MacNutt writes, "In the third century…when adults were
baptized, it was expected that when they rose up out of the baptismal
water, they might prophesy or start praying in tongues."[6]

Tertullian (160–240), who gained the title "Father of Latin Theology,"
wrote about prophecies, words of knowledge, healings, speaking in
tongues, and exorcisms. He addressed those preparing for baptism:
"You blessed ones, for whom the grace of God is waiting, you spread
out your hands…ask your Father, ask your Lord, for the special gift
of his inheritance, the distribution of charisms."[7]

You can read about these manifestations continuing in the writings of Origen (185–284), Novatian (210–280), Cyprian (195–258), and
others. All of these men were well aware of Paul's list of the gifts of
the Spirit, and in no place do they suggest that any of the gifts ceased.
Origen noted that these signs had diminished, and he cited the lack of
holiness and purity among the Christians of his day as the reason for
their diminishing. He noted that Christians cast out demons "merely
by prayer and simple adjurations which the plainest person can use,
because, for the most part, it is unlettered [illiterate] persons who perform this work." He added that exorcism does "not require the power
and wisdom of those who are mighty in argument." In other words,
any Christian could do it.[8]

Cyprian says, "Besides the visions of the night, even in the day-
time, innocent children among us are filled with the Holy Spirit; and
in ecstasies see, and hear, and speak those things by which God is
pleased to admonish and instruct us."[9]

In his *Letter to the Rev. Dr. Conyers Middleton,* John Wesley
writes, "Arnobius tells us 'Christ appears even now to men unpolluted,
and eminently holy, who love him;—whose very name puts evil spirits
to flight, strikes their prophets dumb, deprives the soothsayers of the
power of answering, and frustrates the acts of arrogant magicians.'"[10]
And Arnobius also wrote that Jesus "chose fishermen, artisans, rus-
tics, and unskilled persons of a similar kind, that they being sent
through various nations, should perform all those miracles, without

without any material aids....By the application of His
ed the mark of leprosy....Sores of immense size...He
further feeding on the flesh, by the interposition of
hey, in like manner, compelled the obstinate and mer-
confine itself to a scar."[11]

salem (c. 315–387) claimed that hermits, virgins, and
charisms.[12]

rteaga writes that as the church hierarchy became
gy took over the functions of the charismatically gifted
s the responsibilities of clergy increased, prophetic
by a charismatically gifted person became a threat
he clergy." And, "the Catholic ritual of anointing the
g out of the hands of lay people and institutionalized
o clergy."[13]

ints out that "with the rise of creeds and councils to
y, the definition of a Christian increasingly became
f who intellectually conformed to the creeds and
a matter of who trusted in Jesus and could heal the
ions or do the other mighty works that Jesus sent us

rs

ministry continued among the desert fathers, but
ignificant changes.

es, "In the fourth century there arose a form of
t community in the Egyptian and Palestinian desert
ar-reaching influence in the history of Christianity.
ins who came to these communities wanted to sep-
rom the immorality of the Roman Empire and live
an setting. They dedicated themselves to prayer and
radition of John the Baptist and Elijah."[15]

g, the desert monks were gifted in healing and exor-
gan to succumb to the secular Stoic philosophy of
would focus on Paul's "thorn in the flesh" passage
hat talked about taking up the cross and sharing in
rist. So suffering from illness came to be viewed as
sufferings. "The monks were still willing to pray for

outsiders, but they were not anxious to receive healing prayer themselves," in order that they might partake in the sufferings of Christ.[16]

The founder of Egyptian monasticism was Antony (c. 250–356). According to DeArteaga, "Early in his Christian life Antony heard 1 Corinthians 9:27—*But I buffet my body and make it my slave, lest possibly, after I have preached to others, I myself should be disqualified.* It made a tremendous impression on him and for twenty years he lived as a hermit in prayer and fasting and self-denial. After this season of prayer he emerged to a more public life with several gifts of the Spirit including discernment of spirits and healing. People from all over Egypt came to him with their sick and possessed."[17]

John Crowder writes, "At times, when Antony preached openly the people flocked to hear him, including pagans, who were all struck by the depth of his character. Many were converted, and he was known for working many miracles. He also had open visions, heard the audible voice of God, cast out devils, commanded animals to do things at times, and even caused water to spring up in the desert by his prayer during a drought....Like other Desert Fathers, Antony's life was filled with constant interactions with angels and demons....On several occasions, his cell was supernaturally filled with snakes and reptiles, but after commanding them to leave, they also departed."[18]

Antony warned his fellow monks not to be puffed up with pride because of their spiritual gifts, which was a valid point, but this warning that spiritual gifts can endanger the monk's humility and prayer life became a central theme of later monastic literature. The gifts came to be seen as tools to be used infrequently because they were a danger to a person's holiness.[19]

So, William DeArteaga points out the dilemma: "The traditions of Desert Christianity had produced a double bind on the Catholic. If a Catholic felt he had a ministry of healing, he should not exercise it because it was a threat to his humility. If he exercised it, he was not humble, and therefore his ministry was not valid."[20]

Where did this leave the church? DeArteaga states, "John Cassian [360–435] summed up what he had learned in the desert monasteries about the use of the gifts of the Spirit: *When [the monks] did possess them by the grace of the Holy Spirit, they would never use them, unless perhaps extreme and unavoidable necessity drove them to do so.* And more than one thousand years later, the theology of avoiding the spiritual gifts was codified by St. John of the Cross, a Doctor of the Church, where he wrote that any spiritual manifestations like visions or gifts of healing endangered the believer's quest for spiritual perfection."[21]

This was a significant departure from the New Testament, where Paul said that spiritual gifts were to be "earnestly desired" (1 Cor. 14:1)!

The Post-Nicean Fathers

Ambrose (340–397) was bishop of Milan. In his treatise *Of the Holy Spirit,* Ambrose describes the work of the Trinity in gracing the church with spiritual gifts. He wrote, "You see, the Father and Christ also sets teachers in the churches; and as the Father gives the gifts of healings, so too does the Son give; as the Father gives the gift of tongues, so too has the Son also granted it. In like manner...the Holy Spirit grants the same kind of graces. So, then the Spirit gives the same gifts as the Father, and the Son also gives them."[22]

Francis MacNutt notes that supernatural ministry continued, yet there were further restrictions on this ministry: "From the fifth century on, we read many testimonies of healing. But no longer did the believer talk with the sick person, make up his own prayer tailored to the sick person's need and, together with the laying on of hands, trust that God's power might be transmitted by the human touch. The human need for healing the sick still remained strong as ever. The sick and suffering, in their thronging multitudes, cried out for help, but they were discouraged from going to ministers of healing living on this earth. Instead, they were sent off to shrines filled with the statues of the saints and their relics."[23]

Although it makes many of us Protestants uncomfortable, the fact is that some people did receive healing at these shrines. And there may be biblical precedent for this. In the Catholic church, a relic is the body, part of a body, or part of a possession of a saint—a person known to be filled with the Spirit and documented as having been used by God to perform miracles. In the Old Testament, a dead man came to life when he was quickly thrown into Elisha's tomb and came into contact with Elisha's bones there. A woman was healed by touching

Jesus' garment without Him saying anything to her or touching her in any way. In the Book of Acts, people were healed by touching handkerchiefs and aprons touched by the apostles, and people lined up on the streets, believing that they would be healed by even the shadow of an apostle touching them.

If a person is moving under the anointing of God, that anointing does not work only through a spoken word or touch of the hand, as these biblical examples suggest. And that anointing may rest upon a person's physical remains or possessions (Elisha took up Elijah's mantle) even beyond their death (Elisha's bones).

MacNutt mentions further restrictions: "Eventually only priests were allowed to perform exorcisms. A few centuries later...a priest had to receive permission from his bishop to exorcise someone, and the individual had to be proven to be possessed—a rare occasion!"[24]

When we come to Augustine (354–430), we come to a church father referred to by both supporters and opponents of supernatural ministry today. As DeArteaga puts it, "Probably the most important figure in the formation of the theology of healing (and non-healing) was St. Augustine. He not only sketched what became orthodox Catholic theology, but his writings were read extensively by Martin Luther, John Calvin, and other Reformers. Many of his viewpoints were passed on to Protestantism through the Reformers. Unfortunately he initially affirmed several key errors in the theology of healing and manifestations that were affirmed by later Catholic and Protestant theologians."[25]

Early in his life, Augustine reasoned that the miracles of Jesus were done to prove His authority and who He was. He went on to reason that now that we have the full New Testament, we don't need that miraculous evidence—it's in the book! This line of reasoning is what has been called *cessationism*—that is, the belief that miracles and healing and other supernatural ministry ceased after biblical times. This idea did not originate with Augustine, but he adopted this view as a new Christian and maintained it for most of his life.

DeArteaga points out that then Augustine made a dramatic theological turnaround: "About six years before his death, Augustine rejected cessationism. This was due to a dramatic healing that he witnessed himself. That experience caused him to investigate other reports of healings. By the time that he came to write his last works, *City of God* and *The Retractions*, he enthusiastically affirmed the continued healing ministry of the church."[26] *The Retractions* was written to correct his earlier writings. In that work, he explained that miracles were still common in the Christian community. He was humbly admitting that he was wrong in what he had written previously, and he was wanting to "retract" that wrong teaching.

In his work *The City of God,* which he finished four years before his death, Augustine describes the healing ministry that flowed in his diocese after his acceptance of healing prayer. As bishop, he sought to counteract the reluctance of people to testify of miracles and healings and insisted that people give a witness in church. He began to record the healing miracles reported in his diocese.[27]

In 426, Augustine wrote, "I realized how many miracles were occurring in our own day and which were so like the miracles of old and also how wrong it would be to allow the memory of these marvels of divine power to perish from among our people. It is only two years ago that the keeping of records was begun here in Hippo, and already, at this writing, we have nearly seventy attested miracles."[28]

Eddie Hyatt notes that Augustine reported healings from blindness, cancer, gout, hemorrhoids, demonic spirits, and even raising the dead. He even discusses a phenomenon that he called *jubilation,* which seems to be very similar to what modern charismatics call singing in the Spirit, when the mouth is not able to express in words what the heart is singing.[29]

Unfortunately, influential leaders in the Catholic Church largely adopted Augustine's earlier statements, which he later retracted. They endorsed the idea of cessationism. Having said that, the manifestations of the Spirit continued among some notable people in the Catholic Church, whom I will mention later, like Benedict, Gregory the Great, Bernard of Clairvaux, Dominic, and Francis of Assisi.

Another noteworthy saint who ministered supernaturally was St. Patrick.

About him, Fred and Sharon Wright have written, "Patrick of Ireland [c. 389–461] was a visionary leader who had come to know God as he herded sheep in Northern Ireland. He formed the Celtic

Church, which was not connected at all to the Roman Church in the beginning. The Celtic Church spread the truth of Jesus Christ through a powerful missions thrust from 432 until approximately the middle of the 10th century A.D., when it came under the control of Rome. Their emphasis on being full of the Spirit and being Spirit-led, coupled with healings, signs, and wonders, kept them moving and permeating more and more of what is now Northern and Western Europe. They ventured perhaps even as far as the eastern coast of Canada in their quest to spread the gospel of Christ."[30]

Of his labors, Patrick writes, "I felt all the more His great power within me.... His Spirit is within me and works in me to the present day...nor will I conceal the signs and wonders which the Lord has shown to me.... The Lord also foretells through the prophet, saying: 'And in the last days...I will pour out My Spirit over all flesh and our sons and daughters will prophesy...indeed in those days I will pour out My Spirit.'"[31]

The Middle Ages

Fred and Sharon Wright say of the Benedictines, "In 528, Benedict of Nursia [c. 480–547] established a movement that emphasized a quiet, simple life of order, prayer, and seeking God in reaction to the fallen state that was observable in the city of Rome. Benedictines, as this group became known, also cured the sick, relieved distress, and are said to have even raised the dead."[32]

Richard Riss writes that "in 601, Gregory the Great, bishop of Rome, found it necessary to write to Augustine of Canterbury, exhorting him not to be puffed up with pride that great miracles were taking place during the course of his missionary endeavors in Britain."[33]

Supernatural ministry was not limited to the Roman Catholic Church. Charles Schmitt reveals that in Eastern Orthodoxy, Simeon, a forerunner of Orthodox renewal, wrote, "We are able to manifest the working of miracles and the grace of prophecy and diverse kinds of tongues and interpretation of tongues, helps, and the administration of cities and people and the full knowledge of future blessings, and the gaining of the kingdom of heaven, adoption and the putting on of Christ and the knowing of the mysteries of Christ.... We who are believers are able to know and to believe and say all these things, being taught by the Holy Spirit alone."[34]

Our modern mind at times has difficulty accepting stories of supernatural ministry from the Middle Ages. John Crowder comments, "Tales of medieval miracles sound quite far-fetched to the modern reader; and even the most Spirit-filled Christians are more apt to dismiss them as mythology than as legitimate history. But is God's power not boundless? In an era when society was completely open to manifestations of God's power, it is likely that miracles would have been much more common than today.... If there is a problem with believability, it should only be because of poor record--keeping—but never should we question God's ability or desire to perform the phenomenal. God has always worked frequently and dramatically among men."[35]

Crowder continues, "It is clear that miraculous tales became stretched in the Middle Ages, and wherever there is hype surrounding God's power, criticism will follow. But skepticism was the undercurrent of the Age of Reason, and so every legitimate miracle from the past was thought to be just as phony as the contrived ones. It's as if society jumped from one extreme of believing just about anything to the other extreme of believing nothing."[36]

Eddie Hyatt writes, "During the Middle Ages, a sharp distinction arose between those who performed miracles and those who did not. The monks came to be seen as a spiritual elite with a sort of monopoly on intimacy with God. At the same time, a pronounced bias emerged against the occurrence of miracles among the common people. This bias was clearly demonstrated by the Roman Catholic Church's publication of the Roman Ritual around the year A.D. 1000. It declared, among other things, that speaking in tongues among the common people was to be considered *prima facie* evidence of demon possession. Among the monastics and church hierarchy, however, it could be considered evidence of sainthood!"[37]

Coming into the next millennium, Charles Schmitt writes that Bernard (1090–1153), founder of the monastery at Clairvaux and author of the hymn "Jesus, the Very Thought of Thee," was a Spirit-anointed man: "From all quarters sick persons were conveyed to him by the friends who sought from him a cure."[38] On one day he is reported to have cured nine blind people, ten who were deaf or dumb, and eighteen lame or paralytic. He did this by simply making the sign of the cross over them and they were healed.[39] During a single journey, "Bernard's companions documented 172 blind people healed as well as nearly 200 crippled persons healed. At times, he would be swarmed with crowds, sometimes shuffling in the sick through windows."[40]

Schmitt notes that Hildegard (1098–1179), leader of the Benedictine convent near Bingen on the Rhine, was considered a woman of great spiritual importance in her day. "Scarcely a sick person came to her without being healed," and apparently she sang in tongues, as "concerts in the Spirit" were attributed to her by her peers.[41]

Regarding another great order in the Roman Catholic Church, Fred and Sharon Wright point out that Dominic (1170–1221) established the Dominicans, who moved in signs and wonders, including raising the dead and speaking in tongues.[42] Francis MacNutt relates a story from Dominic's ministry: "A young man named Napoleon was killed in Rome when he fell off a horse. Dominic had the body carried into a chapel and there, in the presence of three cardinals and numbers of priests and nuns, he blessed the corpse and shouted, 'Napoleon, in the name of our Lord Jesus Christ, arise.' Immediately, in the presence of these reliable witnesses, the young man arose, whole and well."[43]

MacNutt notes that supernatural ministry continued among the Dominicans, for one hundred years later, one of Dominic's followers, St. Vincent Ferrer (1350–1419), was not embarrassed to estimate that he had worked three thousand miracles—and of these, 873 were documented by the Church when he was canonized![44]

Francis of Assisi (1182–1226), for whom the current pope is named, established the Franciscan order, where prophecy, miracles, healings, and speaking in tongues were common practices. This order has been considered the most thoroughly charismatic and Holy Spirit–led order that the Catholic Church has ever known.[45] Sometimes infectious gales of laughter would sweep over the early Franciscans during their worship.[46] Anthony of Padua, a member of the Franciscan order, was known for prophetic powers and miracles. At his Lenten series in Padua in 1231, there were 30,000 in attendance at one time, and the response was so great that the number of clergy present was insufficient for the needs of the people.[47]

Francis MacNutt writes that Italian mystic St. Catherine of Sienna (1347–1380) not only healed the sick but also had the extraordinary gift of looking into people's souls and confronting them with their secret sins.[48]

MacNutt writes a fascinating section in his book *Healing Reawakening* on "the royal touch." For seven hundred years, the ancient English and French believed that their kings and queens had the power to heal. They called it "the royal touch." As they saw it in those days, their monarch's healing gift did not depend on his or her goodness but on the fact that they were anointed by God to serve as their king or queen.[49] Not only did everyone then believe in this kind of healing, but they acted upon it in a big way; in both France and England, the monarchs regularly held large healing services! Many testimonies of healing were recorded. Even King Henry VIII held healing services several times a year.[50] In both England and France, the monarch would actually touch each sufferer, as well as say a prayer for him or her, in a prescribed healing ritual. If you have ever prayed for individuals at a healing service, you know how much time and energy you expend and how tired you can get. Most healing evangelists today do not pray for each and every individual in a crowd, and yet the English and French monarchs did: "Each healing service took the better part of two or three entire days. King Louis XIV of France prayed for 3,000 people on Pentecost Sunday 1698. In England Charles II prayed for 23,000 people in a four year span and for some 100,000 in his 25 year reign.... The basic idea was a Christian one, that God was the power behind the healing and the monarch was only a secondary human mediator."[51] Ironically, in England it was *zealous religious reformers* who persuaded the monarchs to stop praying for the sick. In France, it was the *atheistic reformers* who instantly stopped royal healing services by lopping off the king's head.[52] "This era represented the strictest narrowing of the healing ministry. In all of England, only one person could pray for healing! And the same in France.... And no one objected!"[53]

In his book *Saints Who Raised the Dead: True Stories of 400*

Resurrection Miracles, Albert Hebert[54] tells the stories of numerous Roman Catholics who raised the dead and did other miracles in church history. Some of those have already been mentioned above, but Hebert tells about many more. (See Appendix 1, "Raising the Dead in Scripture and History.")

The Reformers

Moving on to the Protestant Reformers, realize that all of the first-generation Reformers were taught Catholic theology. Healing prayer became an established, formal rite of the Church. And only the bishop or priest was permitted to pronounce the prayer over the sick. Most laypeople would not have had the audacity to pray for a friend, or even a family member, to be healed.[55]

Francis MacNutt writes, "In the early Church, bishops would bless oil to be used for anointing the sick, and the laypeople would take it home and use it to anoint each other and pray for their families. Gradually, however, the anointing came to be seen as a special prerogative of the priest, whose anointing came to be considered as a sacrament—the Anointing of the Sick, which laypeople could not minister."[56]

MacNutt further points out that in the ninth century, the sacrament of anointing of the sick became the sacrament of the last anointing. It was no longer for healing but for preparing a person for dying.[57] This enormous change from "everyone can pray" to "only a few can pray," and in limited conditions at that, profoundly influenced the Protestant churches, too, because by the time they appeared on the scene in the sixteenth century, the practice of ordinary people praying for healing had already disappeared. Praying with one another for healing was no longer part of Christian culture.[58]

That same view was later expressed by Jonathan Edwards when revival broke out in his church in Northampton, Massachusetts, in 1734. In spite of many manifestations of the Spirit being demonstrated there, DeArteaga notes that Edwards believed the revival was dampened by, among other things, some persons in the community who had suffered from the "enthusiastic delusion" of believing that laymen were capable of ministering to others. Edwards counseled with one who believed that in the coming revival, the gifts of the Spirit would be released again, and Edwards helped him see his "errors."[59]

John Crowder draws our attention to where the spiritualist William Howitt, in his book *History of the Supernatural*, published in 1863, seemed to hit the nail on the head regarding the modern church's (1863) lack of supernatural power. He said the problem of doubt did not lie in the skepticism of the Age of Enlightenment. He traced it all the way back to the Protestant Reformation. Howitt said Protestantism had built itself by attacking the miracles of Catholicism. "In endeavoring to pull up the tares of false Roman miracle, they have...pulled up the root of faith in miracle, and in the great spiritual heritage of the Church with it," wrote Howitt.[60] And this was the assessment of a spiritualist!

In their efforts in reformation, Luther and Calvin both turned to Augustine for their inspiration, but they read him selectively. Luther did pray for the healing of the sick. He believed in exorcism. And he believed in special revelations of the Spirit. In the fourth verse, second stanza, of his famous hymn "A Mighty Fortress Is Our God," he writes, "The Spirit and the gifts are ours, thru him who with us sideth."

Luther taught on the value of the prophetic in his commentary on Joel 2:28: "For what are all other gifts, however numerous they may be, in comparison with this gift, when the Spirit of God Himself, the eternal God, descends into our hearts, yea, into our bodies, and dwells in us, governs, guides, and leads us? Thus with respect to this declaration of the prophet, prophecy, visions, and dreams are, in truth, one precious gift."[61]

When his lifelong friend and successor, Philipp Melanchthon, lay dying, Luther prayed fervently for him, declaring over him in faith, "Be of good courage, Philipp, you shall not die." Melanchthon recovered and later testified, "I should have been a dead man had I not been recalled from death itself by the coming of Luther." And Luther himself testified, "God gave me back my brother Melanchthon in direct answer to prayer."[62]

When Myconius, the superintendent at Gotha, was in the last stage of consumption, Dr. Luther wrote him: "May God not let me hear so long as I live that you are dead, but cause you to survive me. I pray that earnestly, and will have it granted. Amen." And Myconius began at once to regain strength.[63]

So why isn't there more belief in supernatural ministry among Lutherans and Reformed churches today? Eddie Hyatt tells us: "When he was challenged by Roman Catholic authorities to prove his own authority by miracles, Luther took refuge in the authority of the Scriptures and his own conscience. Miracles, he argued, were particularly suited to the apostolic age and were no longer necessary to vindicate the authority of one who stands on the side of Scripture.... His remarks were taken out of context and codified into a legal system resulting in the Lutheran and Reformed wings of the church harboring a distinct bias against the possibility of present-day miracles. That bias reached its zenith with the publication of *Counterfeit Miracles* by professor B. B. Warfield of Princeton in 1918. In that volume Warfield declared that the Lord had not performed a single miracle on earth since the death of the original twelve apostles and those directly associated with them."[64]

Calvin extended cessationism from Augustine's early understanding—that healing and miracles were no longer operative—to a broader concept: that almost no spiritual experiences were proper for the current age. He reacted against the Catholic mystical tradition of spirituality. He completely denied the validity of spiritual gifts and accepted the five senses and reason as the only reliable way to know truth. Dreams and visions and prophecies were only valid in Bible times. So any current experiences like that were either delusions or demonic.[65]

Calvin wrote, "But that gift of healing, like the rest of the miracles, which the Lord willed to be brought forth for a time, has vanished away in order to make the new preaching of the gospel marvelous forever. Therefore, even if we grant to the full that anointing [for the sick] was a sacrament of those powers which were then administered by the hands of the apostles, it has nothing to do with us, to whom the administering of such powers has not been committed."[66]

Calvinist theologians, like B. B. Warfield at Princeton, carried this even further to assert that after the resurrection of Jesus, demons were banished from the earth so exorcism was unnecessary in the current age.[67] They also claimed that evangelism among the heathen was also an apostolic gift that ceased after biblical times. That delayed large-scale missionary activity among the Reformed churches for almost 150 years.[68] The Divinity Faculty of Wittenberg had denounced missionary advocates as false prophets. "In 1722, the hymnologist Neumeister of Hamburg closed his...sermon by giving out the hymn: 'Go out into the world,' The Lord of old did say; But now; 'where God has placed thee, There he would have thee stay!'"[69] William Carey was told by one of his Calvinistic ministerial brethren, "Sit down, young man, and respect the opinions of your seniors. If the Lord wants to convert the heathen, He can do it without your help."[70]

William DeArteaga points out the dangerous end to which cessationism led Protestant theology: "Protestant Reformers said that miracles happened in biblical times, but they can only be verified by faith in the biblical records, not present-day experiences. They expected the public to believe every miraculous event in the Bible but to reject any modern-day evidence of the miraculous as false. This view made Protestant Reformed theology easy prey for new Enlightenment thinking that wanted to discredit Christianity. Critics exposed the weakness of cessationism by bringing it to its logical conclusion— since no miracles are observable in the present, none took place in the past. Some theologians like Schliermacher developed the *myth interpretation* of Scripture that said the miracles in the Bible were fables or myths that had deep meaning but never occurred historically."[71]

In spite of the cessationism of the Lutheran and Reformed wings of the church, supernatural ministry continued among other Protestants.

Charles Schmitt notes that "starting in 1525, the Anabaptists ('those who baptize again') arose in Zurich, Switzerland. They denounced infant baptism and wanted to gather a visible church of true Christians. It was not unusual for them to dance, fall down under the power of the Spirit, and speak in other tongues. (Contemporary Mennonite author John H. Yoder declared that the Pentecostal movement 'is in our century the closest parallel to what Anabaptism was in the sixteenth.')"[72]

The Protestants in France, starting in the late 1550s, the Huguenots, were not caught up in the cessationism of other Protestants. They insisted that *God has nowhere in the Scriptures concluded himself from dispensing again the extraordinary gifts of His Spirit unto men.*[73] Tongues, visions, prophetic utterances, and other supernatural phenomena were common in their midst. Roberts Liardon writes that among them, "children as young as fourteen months prophesied the word of the Lord in impeccable Parisian French. They often spoke of the angelic song that would be heard in their meetings."[74]

They were persecuted by the Catholic French government, and some fled to England, where they encountered a certain John Wesley who showed a cautious openness to them. When a Dr. Middleton gave Wesley the standard cessationist line that no one since apostolic times had spoken in tongues, Wesley replied, "Sir, your memory fails you again.... It has been heard of more than once, no farther off than the valleys of Dauphiny,"[75] a reference to the French Huguenot prophets.

In the early 1600s in Scotland, among the Presbyterians, as a reaction to the Catholic celebrations of special days, especially Corpus Christi, there developed communions, sacramental occasions, or holy fairs. These were large outdoor gatherings where those attending would hear preaching and take Communion together, sitting at long tables. Leigh Schmidt notes that in 1630, at Kirk of Shotts in Scotland, when John Livingston preached at a "solemn communion" with some other Presbyterians, that reportedly went on "almost day and night, for four or five days." These highly charged meetings "found culmination...in an extraordinary 'down-pouring of the SPIRIT.' As he exhorted the great multitude...many were so overwhelmed...that they fainted away and laid upon the ground 'as if they had been dead.'"[76] These became massive evangelistic gatherings at which manifestations of the Spirit could be readily observed—weeping, fainting, groaning, trembling, rejoicing. These communions were held over a two-hundred-year period.

One of the most famous of these communions was at Cambuslang. On that, Leigh Schmidt comments, "In August 1742 at Cambuslang, a parish a few miles outside of Glasgow, the evangelical awakening in Scotland surged to a new high. There the communion, the second in a month's time, attracted between 30,000 and 50,000 people. There were over twenty-four ministers present, preaching from makeshift pulpits or tents. Still, 'what was most remarkable,' the host minister, William

McCulloch, averred, 'was the spiritual glory of this solemnity, I mean the gracious and sensible presence of God.'"[77]

Schmidt notes evidence of supernatural manifestations of the Spirit at Cambuslang that did not always fit well with Presbyterian theology: "In the preparation disciplines that the lay people participated in leading up to taking communion—fasting, prayer, and contemplation—the people often lapsed into trances, fell down as if dead, heard voices, dreamed dreams, and saw visions. They had very direct and overwhelming encounters with God. These were not ordinary Presbyterian experiences, and some clergy at the time edited these stories out of the history of the Cambuslang revival."[78]

Why is this significant for Methodists? It is this: George Whitefield was at the 1742 revival at Cambuslang. He preached there. And William McCulloch recounted, "While he [Whitefield] was serving some of the tables, he appeared to be so filled with the love of God as to be in kind of ecstasy."[79] Whitefield experienced open-air preaching there, something he would later recommend to John Wesley. And Whitefield saw manifestations of the Spirit there among the people.

The great Cane Ridge Revival of 1801 was actually the Cane Ridge Communion. It was one of these Presbyterian communions imported to Kentucky from Scotland. The camp meetings, even the Methodist camp meetings, began as "communions."

And the "mourner's bench" or "anxious bench"—pews at the front of the church to which would-be converts would be called to "pray through" to full salvation—began at the Presbyterian "communions."[80]

Led by George Fox (1624–1691), the Quakers began in England. God's presence often fell in Fox's meetings as he prayed. Sometimes the building he preached in seemed to rock back and forth with the touch of God. The name *Quaker* was given to this movement because its adherents would tremble when the presence of God fell in their midst. The charismatic gift of new tongues broke out in their meetings.[81] By 1660, the Quakers were the fastest-growing movement in the Western world, with more than 50,000 adherents—and by 1661, more than 4,000 of them were in English jails![82]

John Crowder gives several interesting paragraphs about the Jansenists: "In 18th-century Europe, between the Reformation and the

French Revolution, literally tens of thousands of people began to be swept into trances and shaking with wild manifestations in the open air. These believers could not be termed either Protestant or Catholic and became known as the *Jansenists.*"[83]

"Starting with a prayer meeting at the tomb of one of their leaders in a cemetery in France, the most unusual signs and wonders began to erupt, which mushroomed into a regional explosion. From the beginning, a host of miraculous healings were reported. People also began to experience strange involuntary spasms and contortions of their limbs. The streets were packed with men, women, and children all twisting and writhing. They became known as the *Convulsionaires.*"[84]

These were eventually persecuted by the church and the state. But this became such a massive movement that it took three thousand people just to cover flailing women with blankets so they would not become immodest. The streets and cemetery stayed packed, day and night, for twenty years![85]

Because of the persecution the Jansenists experienced, we hear little about them today. But the Jansenist miracles were the talk of Europe for an entire century. They were the buzz of the Western world, as thousands flocked to see them. They were so widely known and their miracles so well documented and verified that even the skeptical writer Voltaire would not deny their supernatural abilities. Four-inch-thick books were composed of firsthand, eyewitness accounts of their miracles. There were untold numbers of *creative miracles,* such as decayed limbs being restored. The most hardened atheists were converted at this.[86]

As their persecutors came to kill them, the Jansenists were suddenly clothed with an *invincibility* that was utterly supernatural. Vinson Synan says the following: "It appears nothing could harm the convulsionaries. They could not be hurt by the blows of metal rods, chains, or timbers. The strongest of men could not choke them. Some were crucified and afterward showed no trace of wounds. Most mind-boggling of all, they could not even be cut or punctured with knives, swords, or hatchets."[87]

Secular researcher Michael Talbot comments, "Invulnerability was not the only talent the Jansenists displayed during their seizures.

Some could prophesy and were able to discern hidden things. Others could read even when their eyes were closed and tightly bandaged, and instances of levitation were reported. One of the levitators, an Abbe named Bescherand from Montpellier, was so 'forcibly lifted into the air' during his convulsions that even when the witnesses tried to hold him down they could not succeed in keeping him from raising up off the ground."[88]

These manifestations were observed by countless thousands of people, day and night, for a period of many years. Among the Jansenists there developed a kind of sacrament called the *consolamentum*. This was not a baptism of water but of words, which included a laying on of hands and impartation of spiritual gifts. *This was considered a baptism of the Holy Spirit.* Historians note instances of speaking in tongues during this, but many kept the practice secretly guarded so as not to be accused of witchcraft by the mainstream church.[89]

Regarding the Moravians, Eddie Hyatt writes, "In 1727, a Moravian pastor was leading a church meeting when he was overwhelmed by the presence of the Lord and fell to the floor. The entire congregation was overwhelmed by the Spirit and presence of God and sank to the floor with him. After that Moravians began to be filled with the Spirit and prophesy. Supernatural gifts were manifested, miraculous cures were experienced. Some spoke in tongues."[90]

Moravian historian John Greenfield writes, "Church history abounds in records of special outpourings of the Holy Ghost, and verily, the thirteenth of August, 1727, was a day of the outpouring of the Holy Spirit. We saw the hand of God and his wonders, and we were all under the cloud of our fathers, baptized with their Spirit. The Holy Ghost came upon us, and in those days great signs and wonders took place in our midst. From that time, scarcely a day passed but what we beheld His almighty workings amongst us. A great hunger after the Word of God took possession of us so that we had to have three services every day, at 5:00 and 7:30 a.m. and 9:00 p.m. Everyone desired above everything else that the Holy Spirit might have full control.... An overwhelming flood of grace swept us all out into the great ocean of Divine Love."[91]

On August 25, 1727, Count von Zinzendorf called upon homeless

Moravian and bohemian Protestants, whom he had invited to settle on his estate at Herrnhut in Saxony to start a prayer meeting that lasted over one hundred years! He observed that "at this juncture, supernatural gifts were manifested in the church, and miraculous cures were wrought." And historian Greenfield noted that "Christian women and young people were filled with the Spirit and prophesied."[92]

It was Moravian missionaries who sailed to Georgia on the same boat as John Wesley and who had a profound influence on his life. And it was at a Moravian meeting on Aldersgate Street that Wesley felt his heart strangely warmed.

Ann Taves notes the parallels between the Moravians and the Methodists. She writes, "The community at Herrnhut was divided into 'choirs' composed of men and women of all ages, both single and married, that were similar in many ways to Wesley's later 'societies.' Additionally, there were small voluntary groups of five to ten people at the same stage of spiritual development called 'bands,' upon which Wesley modeled his 'bands' and 'class meetings.' The Moravians also celebrated an Agape meal of bread and water that was taken up as the Methodist 'love-feast' and, as inveterate hymn-singers, the Moravians also provided many of the hymns that fueled the Methodist movement, especially in its early stages."[93]

John Arnott reports that Richard Riss has done extensive research into revivals throughout church history. He documents sixty-two different revivals since the 1200s. Many of these had similar manifestations: falling, shaking, visions, trances, and, to a lesser degree, laughing and drunkenness in the Spirit.[94]

Chapter Two

THE METHODISTS IN
ENGLAND AND AMERICA

Is This Methodist?

OR SOME, THIS is a more important question than "Is it biblical?" or "Has it happened before in church history?"

Randy Clark reports that when several Southern Baptist seminary professors of evangelism were asked by phone, "What was the greatest revival in Baptist history?" the response was unanimously, "The Shantung Revival in China." Healing, falling, electricity, laughing in the Spirit, even the raising of the dead is recorded in *The Shantung Revival,* a book by Mary Crawford, one of the Southern Baptist missionaries who experienced this revival firsthand in the early 1930s. In the book are accounts of almost everything that has been characteristic of the Toronto Revival and the Pensacola Outpouring. Unfortunately, most Southern Baptists are not aware of what happened during their greatest revival. Several years ago, the book was reprinted with almost all of the phenomena of the Holy Spirit edited out.[1]

Southern Baptists have "sanitized" their history at this point. They have removed historical accounts that are not consistent with their current theology and practices. Some Presbyterians did the same thing when it came to recording the history of the Cambuslang revival. And some Methodists have done the same "sanitizing" of our history in removing many accounts of the supernatural power and manifestations of the Holy Spirit moving among the Methodists.

So, what about the ministries of Wesley, Whitefield, and Asbury? Is this stuff Methodist?

In his *Journal,* John Wesley writes on Monday, January 1, 1739, the New Year's Day after his Aldersgate Street experience with the Moravians, "About three in the morning, as we were continuing instant in prayer, the power of God came mightily upon us insomuch that many cried out for exceeding joy, and many fell to the ground."[2] Twenty-four-year-old George Whitefield, who was present at this meeting, wrote, "It was a Pentecostal season indeed....We were filled as with new wine...overwhelmed with the Divine Presence."[3]

Wesley wrote on April 17, 1739, "We called upon God to confirm His Word. Immediately one that stood by (to our no small surprise) cried out aloud, with the utmost vehemence, even as in the agonies of death. But we continued in prayer, till a new song was put in her mouth....Soon after two other persons...were seized with strong pain, and constrained to roar for the disquietness of their heart."[4]

Again he wrote, "April 26, 1739—While I was preaching at Newgate....Immediately one, and another, and another sunk to the earth: They dropped on every side as thunderstruck."[5]

Four days later he wrote, "April 30, 1739—We understood that many were offended at the cries of those on whom the power of God came: Among whom was a physician, who was much afraid there might be fraud or imposture in the case. Today one whom he had known for many years was the first...who broke out 'into strong cries and tears.' He could hardly believe his own eyes and ears....But when both her soul and body were healed in a moment, he acknowledged the finger of God."[6]

And a day later, "May 1, 1739—Many were offended again, and, indeed much more than before. For at Baldwin Street my voice could scarce be heard amidst the groaning of some, and the cries of others, calling aloud to Him that is 'mighty to save.'...A Quaker, who stood by, was not a little displeased at the dissimulation of these creatures and was biting his lips and knitting his brows, when he dropped down as thunderstruck. The agony he was in was even terrible to behold. We besought God not to lay folly to his charge. And he soon lifted up his head and cried aloud, 'Now I know thou art a prophet of the Lord!'"[7]

Manifestations of the presence and power of God continued in Wesley's ministry. He wrote, "July 19, 1757—Toward the conclusion of my sermon, the person with whom I lodged was much offended at one who sunk down and cried aloud for mercy. Herself dropped down next and cried as loud as her, so did several others quickly after."[8]

On July 14, 1759, at Everton, he wrote, "The Lord was wonderfully present, more than twenty persons feeling the arrows of conviction. Several fell to the ground; some of whom seemed dead; others, in the agonies of death, the violence of their bodily convulsions exceeding all description. There was also great crying and agonizing in prayer mixed with deep and deadly groans on every side."[9] And at Grandchester on the same day, he wrote, "God had there broken down seventeen persons, last week, by the singing of hymns only; and that a child, seven years old, sees many visions, and astonishes the neighbours with her innocent, awful manner of declaring them."[10] And in a follow-up entry on July 22, he wrote, "Ten more persons were cut to the heart in singing hymns among themselves; and the little child before-mentioned continues to astonish the neighbourhood. A noted Physician came some time ago and closely examined her. The result was, he confessed it was no distemper of mind, but the hand of God."[11]

In a letter to Wesley from Limerick in 1762, reporting on the work of God there, we find, "Many more were brought to the birth. All were in floods of tears, they cried, they prayed, they roared aloud, all of them lying on the ground."[12]

And toward the end of his ministry, at Coleford in 1784, Wesley writes, "When I began to pray, the flame broke out—many cried aloud, many sank to the ground, many trembled exceedingly. But all seemed to be quite athirst for God, and penetrated by the presence of his power."[13] These manifestations were present throughout Wesley's ministry.

On May 9, 1740, Wesley reported an incident that happened ten or eleven years before, where he and his brother, Charles Wesley, took a walk in a meadow intending to sing psalms in praise to God. Just as they started to sing, Charles burst out into loud laughter. Before long, John too was laughing uncontrollably.[14] In his *Second Letter to Bishop Lavingtoni,* Wesley noted the bishop commenting on this event from his *Journal,* having said, "Though I am not convinced that these fits of laughing are to be ascribed to Satan, yet I entirely agree, that they are involuntary and unavoidable." Wesley responded that he entirely agreed with that statement but added, "But I must still go farther: I cannot but ascribe them to a preternatural agent; having observed so many circumstances attending them which cannot be accounted for by any natural causes."[15]

It is important to understand that these experiences are not isolated incidents in Wesley's ministry. They are illustrative of experiences with the supernatural manifestation of the power of God that were frequent throughout his ministry. Readers of Wesley will note less reporting of these later in his ministry, but it is possible that by then they were not unusual enough to report.

Wesley was clearly not a Reformed cessationist. He wrote, "I do not recollect any Scripture wherein we are taught that miracles were to be confined within the limits either of the apostolic age... or any period of time, longer or shorter, even till the restitution of all things."[16]

In his *Journal,* he wrote, "The grand reason why the miraculous gifts were so soon withdrawn, was not only that faith and holiness were well nigh lost; but that dry, formal, orthodox men began even then to ridicule whatever gifts they had not themselves, and to decry them all as either madness or imposture."[17]

In a sermon, he wrote, "It does not appear that these extraordinary gifts of the Holy Ghost were common in the Church for more than two or three centuries.... The real cause was 'the love of many,' almost of all Christians, so called, was 'waxed cold.' The Christians had no more of the Spirit of Christ than the other heathens.... This was the real cause why the extraordinary gifts of the Holy Ghost were no longer to be found in the Christian Church; because the Christians were turned heathens again, and had only a dead form left."[18]

Professor Laurence Wood writes, "It was not uncommon for unusual manifestations (as tears of joy, etc.) to occur in Wesley's and Fletcher's meetings during the years 1770–1792, and Wesley was no longer preoccupied with the fear of fanaticism. *The Arminian Magazine* (begun in 1778) also devoted a whole *section* each month to unusual manifestations of divine providence reported to it by its readers. These were usually listed under sections called 'The Providence of God Asserted' and 'The Grace of God Manifested.' Without indicating a defensive posture, Wesley boldly affirmed the daily providence and miraculous activity of God in the world. Wesley's personal diary records instances of miraculous divine interventions."[19]

And on speaking in tongues, to Dr. Middleton, Wesley wrote, "He who worketh as He will, may, with your good leave, give the gift of tongues where He gives no other; and may see abundant reasons to do so, whether you and I see them or not."[20]

John's brother, Charles, wrote "A Hymn for Pentecost" that is not in our United Methodist hymnal. In the fifth verse he wrote, "Now let us speak with other tongues / the new strange language of Thy love."

Thomas Walsh, a friend and colleague of Wesley, wrote in his journal February 24, 1751, "The influence of His Spirit wrought so powerfully upon me, that my joy was beyond expression." In Walsh's journal on March 8, 1751, he writes, "This morning the Lord gave me a language I knew not of, raising my soul to Him in a wonderful manner."[21]

In his writings, Wesley testified to a belief in demons and spiritual warfare. He believed in and experienced miraculous healings. He believed in the gift of prophecy, visions, and dreams. He testified to the ministry of angels.

In his sermon "On Divine Providence" (written in 1784), Wesley writes, "Admitting then that, in the common course of nature, God does act by general laws, he has never precluded himself from making exceptions to them, whensoever he pleases; either by suspending that law in favour of those that love him. Or by employing his mighty angels: By either of which means he can deliver out of all danger them that trust in him. 'What! You expect miracles then?' Certainly I do, if I believe the Bible: For the Bible teaches me, that God hears and answers prayer: But every answer to prayer is, properly, a miracle."[22]

As late as 1856, British Methodist preacher William Arthur published his book *The Tongue of Fire*, which remained in print for more than a century, and in that book he dismissed the traditional view of cessation and the withdrawal of spiritual gifts by saying, "Whatever is necessary to the holiness of the individual, to the spiritual life and minister gifts of the church, or to the conversion of the world, is as much the heritage of the people of God in the latest days as in the first.... We feel satisfied that he who does expect the gift of healing and the gift of tongues or any other miraculous manifestations of the

Holy Spirit…has ten times more scriptural ground on which to base his expectation than have they for their unbelief who do not expect supernatural sanctifying strength for the believer."[23]

DISCERNING "ENTHUSIASM"

Resting in the Spirit, swooning, falling down as if dead, and other such physical manifestations were some of the reasons that the Methodists were given the derogatory term "enthusiasts." When a Church of England clergyman in Maryland railed against the Methodists and "enthusiasm," a woman in the congregation cried out, "Glory to God! If what I now feel be enthusiasm, let me always be an enthusiast!"[24]

John Cennick, one of Wesley's early associates, claimed that "frequently when none were agitated in the meetings, Wesley prayed, 'Lord! Where are thy tokens and signs?' And I don't remember ever to have seen it otherwise that on his so praying several were seized and screamed out."[25]

One of Wesley's supporters expressed concern over what she perceived to be extreme behavior during a Methodist preaching service. She wrote to Mr. Wesley that "while one of them was preaching, several persons fell down, cried out, and were violently affected." Wesley replied in a letter to Mrs. Parker, January 21, 1784, that "it has pleased the all-wise God for near these fifty years, wherever He has wrought most powerfully, that these outward signs (whether natural or not) should attend the inward work." And he advised her to not interfere with the work of God.[26]

Wesley was not willing to label all manifestations as being completely of God. He said that sometimes they were, sometimes it was a mixture of God and the person, and sometimes it might be the devil. He said, "Perhaps the danger *is*, to regard [the manifestations] too little, to condemn them altogether; to imagine they had nothing of God in them, and were an hindrance to his work.…This should not make us either deny or undervalue the real work of the Spirit. The shadow is no disparagement of the substance, nor the counterfeit of the real diamond."[27]

More than once Wesley asked God to forgive him and his associates for "blaspheming His work among us, imputing it either to nature, to the force of imagination and animal spirits, or even to the delusion of the devil."[28]

Within particular seasons throughout John Wesley's entire life, he saw people weeping, violently shaking, crying out, losing consciousness, falling down, and occasionally becoming uncontrollably agitated during his meetings. In response to one who was concerned about the "strange work" that occurred in his meetings, Wesley testified, "I have seen (as far as a thing of this kind can be seen) very many persons changed in a moment from the spirit of fear, horror, despair, to the spirit of love, joy, and peace; and from sinful desire, till then reigning over them, to a pure desire of doing the will of God. These are matters of fact, whereof I have been, and almost am, an eye or ear witness."

Wesley continued, "I will show you him that was a lion till then, and is now a lamb; him that was a drunkard, and is now exemplarily sober; the whoremonger that was, who now abhors the very garment spotted by the flesh." Wesley judged by the "whole tenor" of their lives and called these people his "living arguments."

He then offered the following remarkable explanation for the outward signs: "Perhaps it might be because of the hardness of our hearts, unready to receive any thing unless we see it with our eyes and hear it with our ears, that God, in tender condescension to our weakness, suffered so many outward signs of the very time when He wrought this inward change to be continually seen and heard among us."[29]

While Wesley was ministering in England, his colleague George Whitefield was ministering in the American colonies. Early in his career, when he was working with Wesley in England and people started to fall, Whitefield protested to Wesley about these behaviors by letter: "I cannot think it right in you to give so much encouragement to these convulsions which people have been thrown into in your ministry. Were I to do so, how many would cry out every night. I think it is tempting God to require such signs."[30]

Later, Whitefield came to confront Wesley about this in person. The day after Whitefield spoke to Wesley about this, while Whitefield was preaching, here is what Wesley records happening in his *Journal* for July 7, 1739: "The next day he had an opportunity of informing himself better: For no sooner had he begun [in the application of his sermon] to invite all sinners to believe in Christ, than four persons sunk down close to him, almost in the same moment. One of them lay without either sense or motion. A second trembled exceedingly. The third had strong convulsions all over his body, but made no noise, unless by groans. The fourth, equally convulsed, called upon God, with strong cries and tears. From this time, I trust, we shall all suffer God to carry on His own work in the way that pleaseth Him."[31] (That is good advice to all of us!)

Wesley was sensitive to the danger of criticizing someone else's spiritual experience. We read in 2 Samuel 6 that David danced himself out of his clothes while bringing the Ark of the Covenant from the house of Obed Edom to Jerusalem and that his wife, Michal, criticized his behavior. We read that she became barren because of this criticism. One of the ways that we become spiritually barren is by criticizing the spiritual experience of another person.

John Crowder writes, "John tells us to 'prove the spirits whether they be of God' (1 Jn. 4:1). He never tells us to test the outward manifestations, but the spirits themselves.... Discernment is not a paranoid hunt for devils in the middle of every manifestation.... Instead, John's admonition was positive and optimistic; he wanted us to constantly be looking for God in every situation, testing spirits to see if they are bringing something of value from Him.... The problem is that paranoia has long masqueraded as the gift of discernment of spirits. Here is another way of explaining it: Instead of trying the spirits 'whether they be of God,' we have tried the spirits whether they be of the devil."[32]

Crowder goes on to say, "We need an extreme tolerance for manifestations. Think of how patient the apostle Paul was with this stuff! When Paul visited Macedonia in Acts 16, a slave girl possessed by a spirit of divination followed him for 'many days.'... Paul allowed this girl to rattle off for *many days* before getting 'greatly annoyed' and casting out her devils.... Paul afforded great leniency with manifestations. Give God room to work, and don't stress out about devils around every corner."[33]

The need for "watchmen on the wall" is often raised in charismatic circles. There is certainly a need for watchmen and watchwomen!

But Crowder clarifies their purpose: "The most important thing is to recognize when the *Lord* is truly moving, so we do not miss out on His fullness. The watchmen on the wall had a twofold responsibility in Old Testament times. They sounded an alarm when they saw the enemy approaching. But this was not their primary task. The greater responsibility was to *watch for the king coming,* so the gates could be opened and the inner chambers prepared for him."[34]

A king would come to one of his cities far more frequently than an enemy. The watchman would be watching more frequently for the coming of the king. Thus, when David writes in Psalm 24:7, "Lift up your heads, O you gates; be lifted up, you ancient doors, that the King of glory may come in," it would have been the watchman who would have cried out this command to open the gates for the coming of the king. And even here, the watchman saw the arrival of the King of glory, not an enemy.

In another place, Crowder asks a poignant question: "Unlike those early disciples, much of the church is so afraid of the demonic, that we won't open up to new ways of spiritual expression with which we are unfamiliar....Is your fear of the demonic greater than your hunger for God?"[35]

Wesley wrote, "I have generally observed more or less of these outward symptoms to attend the beginning of a general work of God...but after a time they gradually decrease, and the work goes on more quietly and silently."[36] But Ann Taves notes, "Methodist historians, wanting to downplay the role of these 'outward symptoms' in the Methodist movement, have wanted to read *disappear* where Wesley wrote *decrease,* but in fact these 'outward symptoms' continued for decades."[37]

(Author's note: When I took my Methodist history course at one of our United Methodist seminaries from a prominent Methodist historian, who wrote the textbook on Methodist history that we used in the course, why did I not learn anything about the supernatural manifestations of the power of God that took place in Wesley's ministry and the ministry of many other early American Methodists? The answer is "bias by the historian." If the historian does not believe in the supernatural or believes that Wesley and the early Methodists were just

ignorant products of their time, believing unscientific and supersti-
tious ideas of their day, then these "facts" would not be included in
their histories.)

Ann Taves goes on to write, "Methodist historian Stephen Gunter
indicates that 'for two centuries students of the Methodist revival have
tended to "play down" Wesley's emphasis on...miraculous interven-
tion.' The fact is, Gunter writes, that '[Wesley] searched incessantly for
testimonies of conversion experiences which would substantiate the
validity of his claim that human experience was a form of proof for
divine activity.' According to Gunter, 'Even Charles, who was more
resistant to this emphasis than John, requested the converts to provide written accounts of their conversion experiences. Scores of letters by converts were sent to Charles fulfilling this request, many of
which have been preserved. A reading of these accounts will destroy
the myth that this emphasis was short-lived.' The tendency to mini-
mize the supernatural aspects of these accounts, as Gunter suggests,
'can probably best be accounted for by recognizing a personal aversion
to such phenomena on the part of scholars themselves.'"[38]

History is not just collecting facts but arranging facts (and leaving
out others) to tell a story. This book on the supernatural among the
Methodists, for instance, does not tell the whole story of the ministry
of Wesley and the Methodists; it brings to the fore facts that support
the theme that there was (and is) a supernatural thread in the fabric
of Methodism.

John Wigger, in his book *Taking Heaven by Storm: Methodism
and the Rise of Popular Christianity in America*, wrote, "In fact, it
may not be an exaggeration to say that this quest for the supernatural in everyday life...was the key theological characteristic of early
American Methodism," and he goes on to say, "While early American
Methodism cannot be reduced to enthusiasm, neither can it be understood without it....Visions, dreams, and supernatural impressions
not only held deep religious meaning but also served to validate the
Methodist system. This kind of militant supernaturalism formed an
integral part of the Methodist message in every region of the post-
revolutionary United States."[39]

GEORGE WHITEFIELD

Whitefield first took to preaching in the open air in Hanham Mount, southeast of Bristol, in one of the worst neighborhoods of the day. Approximately 20,000 poor workers came to hear him, their tears cutting white streaks down their dirty faces and "strong men being moved to hysterical convulsions by God's wondrous power."[40]

By the time Whitefield came to America, his preaching was ordinarily accompanied by people toppling over. Dr. John White writes in his book *When the Spirit Comes With Power,* "Under Mr. Whitefield's sermon, many of the immense crowd that filled every part of the burial ground were overcome with fainting. Some sobbed deeply, others wept silently.... When the sermon was ended people seemed chained to the ground."[41]

At Nottingham, Delaware, on May 14, 1740, twelve thousand people gathered. Thousands cried out under conviction, almost drowning Whitefield's voice. Men and women dropped to the ground as though dead, then revived, then dropped again, as Whitefield continued preaching.[42]

Whitefield's meetings were wild, though not all his listeners were fans. "I was honored with having stones, dirt, rotten eggs, and pieces of dead cats thrown at me," he writes.[43]

In October 1741, the Rev. Samuel Johnson, acting dean of Yale College, wrote an anxious letter to a friend in England regarding a revival sweeping New England led by George Whitefield. In the letter he stated, "But this new enthusiasm, in consequence of Whitefield's preaching through the country and his disciple, has got great footing in the College [Yale].... Many of the scholars have been possessed of it, and two of this year's candidates were denied their degrees for their disorderly and restless endeavors to propagate it.... Not only the minds of many people are at once struck with prodigious distresses upon their hearing the hideous outcries of our itinerant preachers, but even their bodies are frequently in a moment affected with the strangest convulsions and involuntary agitations and cramps, which also have sometimes happened to those who came as mere spectators."[44]

At the Cambuslang revival outside Glasgow, Scotland, in 1742, a large communion celebration was held. It was here that people began falling out in the Spirit by the droves. Whitefield was there and commented, "Such a commotion surely was never heard of, especially at eleven at night. It far outdid all that I ever saw in America. For about an hour and a half there was such weeping, so many falling into deep distress, and expressing it in various ways.... Their cries and agonies were exceedingly affecting."[45]

Whitefield, who was serving some of the tables, was "so filled with the love of God as to be in a kind of ecstasy." At the next revival service, hundreds fell out in the Spirit, along with manifestations of laughter, prophecy, and groaning.[46]

Once when preaching in Yorkshire in 1756, Whitefield stood on a platform erected outside an open window of a church, where he could be heard by those inside as well as the several thousand crowded outside. He read from the text in Hebrews 9:27: "It is appointed for men to die once, but after this the judgment." Suddenly, a "wild, terrifying shriek" came from the audience, as someone suddenly dropped dead. One of the ministers pressed through the crowd, and after a moment of confusion, the body was carried away. After a pause, Whitefield began to loudly read again, "And as it is appointed for men to die once, but after this the judgment." Immediately another screech erupted from a different part of the crowd. A second person had dropped dead after hearing Whitefield's words on death and judgment.[47]

It seems that George Whitefield took to heart Wesley's advice to not judge the manifestations so harshly and to "suffer God to carry on His own work in the way that pleaseth Him."

Whitefield was certain that the low state of the church was principally because of clergy who disguised their spiritual deadness with sound doctrine. He declared that ministers can "preach the gospel of Christ no further than we have experienced the power of it in our own hearts."[48]

FRANCIS ASBURY

Francis Asbury was a very disciplined man who insisted, like Wesley, that camp meetings even on the remotest frontier be conducted in a seemly fashion. Yet his revivals, too, were characterized by swooning, shouting, weeping, and a kind of wild behavior known as "the jerks."[49]

In an episcopal directive issued in December 1802, Asbury bestowed his blessing on the general camp meetings in the Carolinas and Georgia (in which he said "hundreds have fallen and have felt the power of God"[50]).

Asbury also said, "The friends of order may allow a guilty mortal to tremble at God's Word...and the saints to cry and shout when the Holy One of Israel is in the midst of them. To be hasty in plucking up the tares is to endanger the wheat."[51]

Wigger comments, "Asbury recognized that the enthusiasm so endemic to American Methodism was not an unfortunate anomaly but the very lifeblood of the movement."[52] He once urged one of his preachers, "Feel for the power; feel for the power, brother."[53]

Francis MacNutt writes in his book *Overcome by the Spirit*, "In summary, it seems that the preaching in the Protestant Church that has had the most profound and lasting effect in both England and the United States has also been accompanied by listeners being overcome in the Spirit. The greatest preachers in nineteenth-century England all regularly saw people fall over in their services: among Anglicans, John Wesley; among Methodists, George Whitefield and Francis Asbury; among Congregationalists, Jonathan Edwards; among Presbyterians, Charles Finney and Barton Stone; and of course numerous Quakers and Shakers."[54]

THOMAS RANKIN

Sometime after his conversion, Thomas Rankin went to hear Wesley preach for the first time. "When we came within the sound of your voice," he wrote Wesley, "I was so struck with the power of God, that if I had not held fast by Dr. Watson's arm, I should have fallen to the ground."

Thomas Rankin was converted after a series of dreams and visions. He was sent by Wesley as a missionary to America. He was appointed by Wesley as general superintendent or superintendent of the American Societies and led the first annual conference in Philadelphia, July 14, 1773, which was the first annual conference ever held in America.

Reflecting in his *Diary* on a gathering in 1774, Rankin wrote, "it seemed as if the very house shook with the mighty power and glory of

Sinai's God. Many of the people were so overcome that they were ready to faint and die under His almighty hand. For about three hours, the gale of the Spirit thus continued to break upon the dry bones.... As for myself, I scarce knew whether I was in the body or not and so it was with all my brethren."[55]

Thomas Rankin was not initially comfortable with the emotions demonstrated by the early American Methodists in their meetings. Commenting on their emotional expressions, Laurence Wood writes, "Some of Wesley's assistants, such as Thomas Rankin who had gone to America as a Methodist missionary, had considerable difficulty containing the emotional responsiveness of their American hearers. It was normal for his American hearers to weep loudly and cry out with shouts of joy, despite the fact that he made deliberate attempts to keep them quiet. Emotional displays were a prominent feature of early American Methodism, and phenomenal conversions and sanctifications were reported in the tens of thousands which involved considerable emotional expression. These Pentecost-like meetings were regularly described by the early Methodists as 'the demonstration and power of the Spirit' and 'a great outpouring of the Spirit.' And there is no indication that Wesley ever tried to persuade Asbury or Coke to put a stop to the emotionalism which was typical of early American Methodism."[56]

Rankin records in 1776, "Now when the power descended, hundreds fell to the ground, and the house seemed to shake with the presence of God."[57]

MANIFESTATIONS AMONG THE EVANGELICALS AND UNITED BRETHREN

Martin Boehm

One of the founders of the German-speaking United Brethren, Martin Boehm, was removed as a bishop among the Mennonites because of his association with Methodists. He allowed the Methodists to form a class in his house. He invited preachers (including English-speaking Methodists) to preach on his property. Methodist lay preacher Benjamin Abbott described a meeting at Martin Boehm's, saying:

Next morning, I set out with about twenty others for my appointment, where we found a large congregation. When I came to my application, the power of the Lord came in such a manner that the people fell all about the house, and their cries might be heard afar off. This alarmed the wicked, who sprang for the doors in such haste that they fell one over another in heaps. The cry of mourners was so great, I thought to give out a hymn to drown the noise, and desired one of our English friends to raise it. But as soon as he began to sing, the power of the Lord struck him, and he pitched under the table, and there lay like a dead man. I gave it out again and asked another to raise it. As soon as he attempted, he fell also....Mr. Boehm, the owner of the house, and a preacher among the Germans, cried out, "I never saw God in this way before." I replied, this is a Pentecost, father. "Yes, be sure," said he, clapping his hands. "A pentecost, be sure!"[58]

Henry Boehm

Henry Boehm, one of Francis Asbury's longtime traveling companions and the son of Martin Boehm, co-founder of the United Brethren Church, was convinced that informal small group gatherings in rural cabins or in village class meetings did more to advance Methodism than better-known public meetings. "It is not generally known, wrote Boehm, that the greatest displays of divine power and the most numerous conversions were in private houses, in prayer meetings."[59]

Henry Boehm wrote about the response to his preaching in his journal for July 5, 1801, "My soul was filled with the powers of the upper work. Many felt the effects of the same: some fell to the floor, others leapt for joy, and mourners [were] crying for mercy....Some were enabled to shout redeeming love."[60]

Jacob Albright

Jacob Albright, the founder of the German-speaking Evangelical Association, gathered his flock in 1802 for the first of many Great Meetings. Converts expressed their joy in a variety of ways. Outbreaks of shouting, stamping in rhythm, or fainting often accompanied his passionate and persuasive preaching. To Albright, the emotional outbursts of the frontier camp meeting implied the presence and power of the Holy Spirit and of true religion. To the Lutheran and Reformed churchpeople, this display of emotion was offensive, and Albright's followers were regularly mocked as "Bush Meeting Dutch," "holy jumpers," knee-sliders, and foot-stampers.[61]

Early Albright meetings were consistently called "Pentecost meetings." The theme of Pentecost appears in other areas of early Evangelical and United Brethren doctrine and theology. For example, the Evangelicals' *Book of Doctrine and Discipline* (1809) described sanctification as experienced in their early "Pentecostal" meetings as a "baptism of fire," which produced a "powerful outpouring of the Holy Spirit." Although the journal of John Seybert, the Francis Asbury of the Evangelicals, makes reference to different modes of baptism, the emphasis clearly falls on the "baptism in the Spirit."[62]

John Seybert always considered it a mark of success when emotions were aroused and people wept or shouted. Evangelicals agreed that "a child of God needs no further argument that Christ is God than that he feels Him in his soul as the living power of God." Jacob Vogelbach, a promising young minister who formed the first missionary society in 1838 and frequently contributed to the church's German periodical, left the church because of his opposition to boisterous worship.[63]

Jason Vickers notes that "in contrast with the Methodist Articles of Religion...the Evangelical United Brethren appear incapable of writing a single statement in their Confession of Faith without at least some reference to the Holy Spirit."[64] Eight out of sixteen articles in the Confession of Faith include references to the Holy Spirit. By contrast, only three out of the twenty-five Articles of Religion do so. The weight given to the Person and work of the Holy Spirit in the Confession of Faith by comparison with the Articles of Religion is truly stunning.[65]

Methodist Local Pastors and Lay Preachers

Manifestations of the Spirit were witnessed as part of the ministries of Wesley, Whitefield and Asbury, Boehm and Albright—some of Methodism's "big guns." But understand that a belief in and openness toward the supernatural manifestation of the power of God was a characteristic of American Methodism as it spread in our country.

Such manifestations were common among the lesser-known American Methodist preachers as well.

While itinerating near Wilmington, Delaware, in the early 1780s, Benjamin Abbott discovered that some feared to sit too near him, having been informed that people on the circuit fell like dead men when he preached. He presided over some of the most explosive Methodist meetings on record. People fainting during his sermons was the hallmark of his career. On one occasion, a "young man was struck to the floor, and many said that he was dead." After three hours, even Abbott became alarmed. Eventually the man revived, "praising God for what He had done for his soul."[66]

James P. Horton was a sometime shoemaker, sometime preacher, and all-time enthusiast known as "Crazy Horton." Following his conversion, Horton spent the next 30 years dividing his time between making shoes to support his wife and thirteen children and preaching wherever he felt led to go. His meetings were filled with shouting, falling, and fervent prayers, and his life with supernatural impressions and prophetic dreams. He was a proponent of divine healing, believing that he himself had been miraculously cured on at least two occasions. One woman went so far as to lock herself in her room when she heard that "Crazy Horton" would be attending a meeting in her house.[67]

There was a one-time itinerant preacher and later physician named John A. Granade who was known as the "wild man" during his preaching days. His brief career was so spectacular that crowds began to follow him from place to place. Some claimed that Granade had a secret powder that he threw over the people to enchant them, and others believed he worked "some secret trick by which he threw them down." At one meeting, so many people fainted and lay in such heaps that it was feared they would suffocate.[68]

On New Year's Day 1801, on the Delmarva Peninsula, a preacher named Thomas Smith was preaching at the home of Thomas Burton, and Burton described what happened by saying, "At the very commencement of the meeting, the Spirit of the Lord came as a rushing mighty wind—the people fell before it and lay in heaps all over the floor. The work continued all night, nor did it stop in the morning, but continued for thirteen days and nights without interruption."[69]

Itinerant preacher William Jessop writes about a prayer meeting he was a part of: "At the end of the meeting the blessed Samaritan passed us by and paid us a glorious visit. The Holy Ghost descended upon us in a mighty rushing wind, and the glory of God filled the house where we were. The shout of a king was in the midst, and many souls rejoiced in the Lord."[70]

There were times when Methodists would pray in one place and the power of God would fall in another place, often miles away. William Keith wrote, "Once they all joined in prayer for a revival of religion in the neighborhood, and at the very same hour the people in their own houses and fields were slain by the power of God. I then began to conclude that this could not be the work of imagination, for these people a mile off, who knew nothing of the meeting, were slain as they were about their work on the very time when those persons prayed for them."[71] (Another example of this can be found in the testimony of Austin Taft in Appendix 2.)

In a 1787 Methodist revival, the preachers could not quiet down the congregation enough to speak, amid all the praises and shouting, until finally they gave up. At the height of the noise, eleven rafters broke in the roof, without anyone noticing it amid the commotion.[72]

John Wigger writes about the extent to which a belief in the supernatural power and activity of God permeated early Methodism: "Perhaps no group had a more enduring attachment to militant Methodist supernaturalism than African-American women.... Since most Methodists believed in the reality of divinely inspired impressions, dreams, and visions, it was not so easy to protest when women, be they white or African-American, manifested such experiences in acceptable and apparently authentic forms. Zilpha Elaw, a black female Methodist, testified of an experience where Jesus appeared to her in a barn. She writes: 'At the time when this occurrence took place, I was milking in the cow stall. And the manifestation of his presence was so clearly apparent that even the beast of the stall turned her head and bowed herself upon the ground.' Jarena Lee records numerous instances of supernatural impressions, dreams, and visions. She believed that God gave her these 'uncommon impressions' to make up for her lack of formal education. She not only had frequent prophetic dreams and visions but also claimed to have an extraordinary gift of healing along with other supernatural powers."[73]

Valentine Cook, Noah Fidler, Philip Gatch, and Joshua Thomas gained reputations as healers whose prayers sometimes brought miraculous results. James P. Horton's, Sampson Maynard's, and Billy Hibbard's autobiographies are filled with stories of dreams, impressions, shouting, and divine healing. Hibbard even includes an account of a woman apparently raised from the dead.[74]

Wigger summarizes, "It may not be an exaggeration to say that this quest for the supernatural in everyday life was the most distinctive characteristic of early American Methodism."[75] (That idea was never mentioned in the seminary course in Methodism that I took!)

Methodist historian Ann Taves says much the same thing as historian John Wigger: "A striking feature of the Methodist accounts was their continual reference to manifestations of the power of God or the outpouring of the Spirit. In his 'Brief Narrative of the Revival of Religion in Virginia,' Devereaux Jarratt said that as early as 'the year 1765, the power of God was...sensibly felt by a few.' In 1770 and 1771, there was 'a more considerable outpouring of the Spirit.' With the arrival of Methodist itinerant Robert Shadford in the winter of 1776, 'the Spirit of the Lord was poured out in a manner we had not seen before.' Over and over, Methodists' accounts of revivals in the 1770s and 1780s refer to the power of God being manifest in their assemblies. Falling to the ground, crying out, and shouting for joy came to be identified by many as specific manifestations of God's presence in their midst."[76]

Lester Ruth also affirms John Wigger's highlighting of the centrality of the supernatural among early American Methodists: "The supernatural realm and the possibility of having an ecstatic experience within it were not on the periphery of their piety. These things occupied the center of their spirituality until well into the nineteenth century. Methodists expected and desired encounters with God and other spiritual beings through visions, dreams, miracles, signs, and wonders. This supernatural quality saturated even their regular religious life in times of prayer and worship as Methodists shouted, fell, and danced in overwhelming experiences of God's wrath, grace, and presence."[77]

Methodists grew faster in Virginia than anywhere else in America. By 1776, half of all the Methodists in America were in Virginia. The Virginia revival of 1773–1776 was the first instance of a Pentecostal-like religious revival in the nation and was a direct antecedent of the frontier Kentucky revivals of 1800. From this stronghold in Virginia, Methodists began their successful growth that eventually spread over the entire continent.[78]

Nathan Bangs described a great revival that swept through Maryland, Delaware, Pennsylvania, Vermont, Connecticut, and New Hampshire and stated "that most of the preachers had received a new baptism of the Holy Spirit—like that which had been showered upon Calvin Wooster, and others in Canada, the preceding year (1799); and wherever they went they carried the holy fire with them, and God wrought wonders by their instrumentality."[79]

The growth of this "heart religion," as Wesley termed it, was not just part of frontier life; it was part of urban life as well. The message of the Methodists had great appeal to the poor and downtrodden. One Congregational minister commented on the Methodist way that was gaining converts daily: "They are constantly mingling with the people, and enter into all their feelings, wishes, and wants; and their discourses are on the level with the capacity of their hearers, and addressed to their understanding and feelings, and produce a thrilling effect, while our discourses shoot over their heads and they remain unaffected.... They reach a large class of people that we do not. The ignorant, the drunken, the profane listen to their homespun but zealous...discourses."[80]

Lester Ruth points out that "exuberant religious expression has often been too closely linked with the so-called frontier regions of early America [Kentucky and Tennessee] and with the start of the Second Great Awakening." And he argues that these were widespread phenomena among Methodists before the beginning of the Awakening in the nineteenth century.[81]

METHODISTS AND HEALING

John Wesley believed in divine healing, prayed for divine healing on a number of occasions, and testified to some cases of supernatural healings as a result of prayer.

In his *Journal*, Wesley wrote, "March 31, 1742. In the evening I called upon Ann Calcut. She had been speechless for some time; but almost as soon as we began to pray, God restored her speech: She then witnessed a good confession indeed. I expected to see her no more. But from that hour the fever left her; and in a few days she arose and walked glorifying God."[82]

Again: "October 16, 1778. Immediately after, a strange scene occurred. I was desired to visit one who had been eminently pious, but had now been confined to her bed for several months, and was utterly unable to raise herself up. She desired us to pray, that the chain might be broken. A few of us prayed in faith. Presently she rose up, dressed herself, came down stairs, and I believe had not any farther complaint."[83]

And again: "May 31, 1785. At eleven I preached in the avenue again.... Afterwards a decent woman, who I never saw either before or since, desired to speak with me; and said, 'I met you at Caladon. I had then a violent pain in my head for four weeks; but was fully persuaded I should be well, if you would lay your hand on my cheek; which I begged you to do. From that moment I have been perfectly well.' If so, give God the glory."[84]

John Wesley saw his horse healed three times as a result of prayer.

Theologian John Fletcher was the most influential person in Methodism next to John and Charles Wesley. He arrived at the conference for Methodist preachers at Bristol in 1777 near death. John Wesley knelt at his side, and all the preachers joined him. Wesley prayed for Fletcher's restoration to health and a longer ministerial career. Mr. Wesley closed his prayer with this prophecy: "He shall not die, but live, and declare the works of the Lord." Mr. Fletcher did recover and lived another eight years.[85]

Jarena Lee not only had frequent prophetic dreams and visions, but she also claimed to have an extraordinary gift of healing along with other supernatural powers.[86]

As has already been stated, Valentine Cook, Noah Fidler, Philip Gatch, and Joshua Thomas gained reputations as healers whose prayers sometimes brought miraculous results. And, James P. Horton's, Sampson Maynard's, and Billy Hibbard's autobiographies are filled with stories of dreams, impressions, shouting, and divine healing. Hibbard even includes an account of a woman apparently raised from the dead.[87]

Henry Boehm recorded a divine healing of his brother's little daughter that he experienced.[88]

Crucial for the beginning of the healing movement was Ethan O. Allen, who was healed of tuberculosis by the prayer of faith at a Methodist class leaders' meeting in 1846. After receiving entire sanctification, he said, "Brethren, if you will pray for me, I believe that this mighty power that has come upon me will heal my lung." Although the class leaders were reluctant to comply with this request since it was not part of their normal practice, they did so based on their knowledge of Mark 16:17–18. To their amazement, Allen was healed "instantly and perfectly." After his healing, Allen took it upon himself to visit poorhouses, where he prayed for the sick and continued a ministry of healing throughout the eastern United States for fifty years.[89]

Then there is this interesting story of the healing of Bishop Simpson, of the M. E. church, that involved not only prayer for healing but a word of knowledge: "In the fall of 1858, whilst visiting Indiana, I was at an annual conference where Bishop Janes presided. We received a telegram that Bishop Simpson was dying. Said Bishop Janes: 'Let us spend a few moments in earnest prayer for the recovery of Bishop Simpson.' We knelt to pray. William Taylor, the great California street-preacher, was called to pray; and such a prayer I never heard since. The impression seized upon me irresistibly: *Bishop Simpson will not die.* I rose from my knees perfectly quiet. Said I: 'Bishop Simpson will not die.' 'Why do you think so?' 'Because I have had an irresistible impression made upon my mind during this prayer.' Another said: 'I have the same impression.' We passed it along from bench to bench, until we found that a very large proportion of the conference had the same impression. I made a minute of the time of day, and when I next saw Simpson, he was attending to his daily labor. I inquired of the bishop: 'How did you recover from your sickness?' He replied: 'I cannot tell.' 'What did your physician say?' 'He said it was a miracle.' I then said to the bishop: 'Give me the time and circumstances under which the change occurred.' He fixed upon the day and the very hour, making allowance for the distance—a thousand miles away—that the preachers were engaged in prayer at this conference. The physician left his room and said to his wife: 'It is useless to do anything further; the bishop must die.' In about an hour he returned, and started back, inquiring: 'What have you done? 'Nothing,' was the reply. 'He is recovering rapidly,' said the physician. 'A change has occurred in the disease within the last hour beyond anything I have ever seen; the crisis is past, and the bishop will recover.' And he did."[90]

METHODISTS AND DELIVERANCE

John Wesley believed in a real devil, demons, and the need for people to be delivered from the power of the devil. He had several encounters with persons who were "demonized."

Dr. Robert Webster has written an article about John Wesley, demon possession, and exorcism. In it, he argues that Wesley was very much aware of the public debate about demons and exorcism as modern science was rising. Webster wrote, "Wesley was familiar with both sides of the debate, and although sensitive to the discoveries of science, he was nonetheless resistant to abandon the belief in diabolical evil or demonic possession. According to Wesley, the idea of possession was corroborated by Scripture and substantiated by human testimony. The elimination of belief in witchcraft and demonic possession would exclude adherence to the Scripture, too."[91]

Webster points out that the Wesley family experienced a poltergeist in the Epworth rectory that they named "Old Jeffrey" for a period of ten years.[92]

Wesley wrote sermons on good angels[93] and evil angels.[94]

In his *Journal,* he wrote, "Dec. 5, 1738. At St. Thomas' was a young woman, raving mad, screaming and tormenting herself continually. I had a strong desire to speak to her. The moment I began she was still. The tears ran down her cheeks all the time I was telling her, 'Jesus of Nazareth is able and willing to deliver you.' O where is faith upon earth? Why are these poor wretches left under the open bondage of Satan? Jesus, Master! Give thou medicine to heal their sickness; and deliver those who are now also vexed with unclean spirits!"[95]

Then, on May 2, 1739:

> I did not mention J—n H—n, a weaver who was at Baldwin-street the night before....Being informed that people fell into strange fits at the Societies, he came to see and judge for himself. But he was less satisfied than before; insomuch that he went about to his acquaintance, one after another, till one in the morning, and labored above measure to convince them it was a delusion of the devil. We were going home, when one met us in the street, and informed us that J—n H—n was fallen raving mad. It seems he had sat down to dinner, but had a mind first to end a sermon he had borrowed on "Salvation by Faith." In reading the last page he changed color, fell off his chair, and began screaming terribly, and beating himself against the ground. The neighbors were alarmed and flocked together to the house. Between one and two, I came in and found him on the floor, the room being full of people, whom his wife would have kept without but he cried aloud, "No, let them all come; let all the world see the just judgment of God." Two or three men were holding him as well as they could. He immediately fixed his eyes upon *me*, and, stretching out his hand, cried, "Ay, this is he who I said was a deceiver of the people. But God has overtaken me." I said, "It was all a delusion, but this is no delusion." He then roared out, "O thou devil! Thou cursed devil! Yea, thou legion of devils! Thou canst not stay. Christ will cast thee out. I know His work is begun. Tear me to pieces if thou wilt; but thou canst not hurt me." He then beat himself against the ground again, his breast heaving at the same time as in the pangs of death, and great drops of sweat trickling down his face. We all betook ourselves to prayer. His pangs ceased, and both his body and soul were set at liberty.[96]

And on Sunday May 20, 1739: "A young man sunk down as one dead; but soon began to roar out, and beat himself against the ground, so that six men could scarcely hold him. His name was Thomas

Maxfield. Except J—n H—n, I never saw one so torn of the evil one. Meanwhile many others began to cry out to the 'Saviour of all' that he would come and help them, insomuch that all the house (and indeed all the street for some space) was in an uproar. But we continued in prayer; and before then the greater part found rest to their souls."[97]

Later that same year, Wesley wrote in his journal about deliverances over a five-day period:

> Tuesday, Oct. 23, 1739. At eleven I preached at Bearfield to about three thousand, on nature, bondage, and adoption. Returning in the evening I was exceedingly pressed to go back to a young woman in Kingswood.... She was nineteen or twenty years old; but, it seems, could not write or read. I found her on the bed, two or three persons holding her. It was a terrible sight. Anguish, horror, and despair, above all description, appeared in her pale face. The thousand distortions of her whole body showed how the dogs of hell were gnawing at her heart. The shrieks intermixed were scarce to be endured. But her stony eyes could not weep. She screamed out, as soon as words could find their way, "I am damned, damned; lost forever. Six days ago you might have helped me. But it is past. I am the devil's now. I have given myself to him. His I am. Him I must serve. With him I must go to hell. I cannot be saved. I will not be saved. I must, I will, I will be damned." She then began praying to the devil. We began, "Arm of the Lord, awake, awake!" She immediately sunk down as asleep; but, as soon as we left off, broke out again with inexpressible vehemence, "Stony hearts, break! I am a warning to you. I am damned, that you may be saved." She then fixed her eyes on the corner of the ceiling, and said, "There he is; aye, there he is; come, good devil come. Take me away. I am yours. Come just now. Take me away." We interrupted her by calling again upon God: on which she sunk down as before; and another young woman began to roar out as loud as she had done. My brother now came in, it being about nine o'clock. We continued in prayer past eleven, when God in a moment spoke peace into the soul, first of the first tormented, and then of the other. And they both joined in singing praise to Him who had "stilled the enemy and the avenger."

Oct 25, 1739. I was sent for to one in Bristol, who was taken ill the evening before....She lay on the ground, furiously gnashing her teeth, and after a while roared aloud. It was not easy for three or four persons to hold her, especially when the name of Jesus was named. We prayed, the violence of her symptoms ceased, though without a complete deliverance.

In the evening, being sent for to her again, I was unwilling, indeed, afraid, to go: Thinking it would not avail, unless some who were strong in faith were to wrestle with God for her. I opened my Testament on those words, "I was afraid, and went and hid thy talent in the earth." I stood reproved, and went immediately. She began screaming before I came into the room; then broke out into a horrid laughter, mixed with blasphemy, grievous to hear....My brother coming in, she cried out, "Preacher! Field preacher! I don't love field preaching." This was repeated two hours together, with spitting and all the expressions of strong aversion.

We left her at twelve, but called again about noon on Friday, 26. And now it was that God showed He heareth the prayer. All her pangs ceased in a moment: She was filled with peace, and knew that the son of wickedness was departed from her.

Saturday 27. I was sent for to Kingswood again, to one of those who had been so ill before. A violent rain began just as I set out, so that I was thoroughly wet in a few minutes. Just at that time, the woman (then 3 miles off) cried out, "Yonder comes Wesley, galloping as fast as he can." When I was come, I was quite cold and dead, and fitter for sleep than prayer. She burst out into a horrid laughter, and said, "No power, no power; no faith, no faith. She is mine; her soul is mine, I have her, and will not let her go."

We begged of God to increase our faith. Meanwhile her pangs increased more and more; to that one would have imagined by the violence of the throes, her body must have been shattered to pieces One who was clearly convinced this was no natural disorder, said, "I think Satan is let loose. I fear he will not stop here," and added, "I command thee, in the name of the Lord Jesus, to tell if thou hast commission to torment any other soul?" It was immediately answered, "I have. L—y C—r, and S—y J—s." (Two who lived at some distance, and were then in perfect health.)

We betook ourselves to prayer again; and ceased not, till she began, about six o'clock, with a clear voice, and composed, cheerful look,—*Praise God, from who all blessings flow.*

Sun. 28—I preached once more at Bradford, at one in the afternoon....Returning in the evening, I called at Mrs. J—'s, in Kingswood. S—y J—s and L—y C—r were there. It was scarce a quarter of an hour, before L—y C—r fell into a strange agony; and presently after, S—y J—s. The violent convulsions all over their bodies were such as words cannot describe. Their cries and groans were too horrid to be borne; till one of them, in a tone not to be expressed, said, "Where is your faith now? Come, go to prayers. I will pray with you. 'Our Father, which art in heaven.'" We took the advice, from whomsoever it came, and poured out our souls before God, till L—y C—r's agonies so increased, that it seemed she was in the pangs of death. But in a moment God spoke: She knew his voice; and both her body and soul were healed.

We continued in prayer till near one, when S—J—'s voice was also changed, and she began strongly to call upon God. This she did for the greatest part of the night. In the morning we renewed our prayers, while she was crying continually, "I burn! I burn! O what shall I do? I have a fire within me. I cannot bear it. Lord Jesus! Help!" Amen, Lord Jesus! When thy time is come.[98]

Exorcism was not just practiced by Wesley. Other Methodists in the connexion did it as well, in spite of the fact that clergy in the Church of England appeared to have abandoned the practice. Robert Webster cites the example of George Lukins. Lukins was a forty-four-year-old tailor who suffered from demonization for eighteen years. News about him appeared in the public newspapers. On Friday, June 13, 1788, John Valton, a Methodist steward, and others gathered at Temple Church in Bristol to exorcize the demon. They prayed and sang for nearly two hours, and Lukins was set free.[99]

METHODISTS' BELIEF IN THE JUDGMENT OF GOD

Wesley believed that, at times, God punished people with sickness and death for their opposition to the truth of God and the Methodists. Here are some examples from his *Journal:*

> October 23, 1740. I was informed of an awful providence. A poor wretch, who was here last week, cursing and blaspheming, and laboring with all his might to hinder the word of God, had afterwards boasted to many, that he would come again on Sunday, and no man should stop his mouth then. But on Friday God laid His hand upon him, and on Sunday he was buried.[100]

> July 15, 1744. I went to Bedlam, at the repeated request of Mr. S—, who had been confined there above two years. This was the person who, while he was speaking against my brother and me to the society at Kingswood, was in a moment struck raving mad. But it seems God is at length entreated for him, and has restored him to a sound mind.[101]

> June 9, 1752. I preached at six to abundance of people near Ewood; and with an uncommon blessing. Hence we rode to Todmorden. The Minister was slowly recovering from a violent fit of a palsy, with which he was struck immediately after he had been preaching a virulent sermon against the Methodists.[102]

People also sometimes dropped dead in George Whitefield's meetings. Once, while preaching in Yorkshire from the Hebrews 9:27 text, "It is appointed unto man once to die," a wild, terrifying shriek came from the audience. One of his ministers pressed through the crowed and cried, "Brother Whitefield, you stand among the dead and the dying, an immortal soul has been called into eternity, the destroying angel is passing over the congregation. Cry aloud and spare not!" After a moment's silence, he began again, only to hear a second shriek and a second one die. After that, the entire mass of the people seemed overwhelmed by his appeal.[103]

Circuit rider Peter Cartwright interpreted the "jerks" as a judgment of God. He said, "I always looked upon the jerks as a judgment sent from God, first, to bring sinners to repentance, and, secondly, to show professors that God could work with or without means, and that He could work over and above means, and do whatsoever seemeth to Him good, to the glory of His grace and the salvation of the world."[104]

Cartwright gave an example of a large drunken man who came to a meeting to disrupt, got the "jerks," and ended up dying: "The jerks were very prevalent.... This large man cursed the jerks, and all religion. Shortly afterward he took the jerks, and he started to run, but he jerked so powerfully he could not get away. He halted among some saplings, and, although he was violently agitated, he took out his bottle of whiskey, and swore he would drink the damned jerks to death; but he jerked at such a rate he could not get the bottle to his mouth, though he tried hard. At length he fetched a sudden jerk, and the bottle struck a sapling and was broken to pieces, and spilled his whiskey on the ground. There was such a great crowd gathered round him, and when he lost his whiskey he became very much enraged, and cursed and swore very profanely, his jerks still increasing. At length a very violent jerk, snapped his neck, fell, and soon expired, with his mouth full of cursing and bitterness."[105]

TRANCES, VISIONS, HEAVENLY VISITATIONS, AND DREAMS AMONG THE METHODISTS

Lester Ruth comments that "Methodists often relied on dreams for guidance, comfort, and discernment of God's hand in their circumstances."[106]

A great many early Methodists believed in the efficacy of prophetic dreams, visions, and supernatural impressions and were not afraid to base everyday decisions on such phenomena.[107] Freeborn Garrettson noted that many "thought the Methodists could work miracles." Indeed, only a few months earlier, in Delaware, he had prayed for rain to end "a great drought with the result that 'a few minutes after the congregation was dismissed, the face of the sky was covered with blackness, and we had a plentiful shower; which greatly surprised and convinced the people.'" Though others scoffed at looking to dreams and visions for guidance, Garrettson defended the practice, stating, "I know, that both sleeping and waking, things of a divine nature have been revealed to me."[108]

Benjamin Abbott had two striking dreams seven years prior to his conversion, one in which he died and went to hell and another in which he journeyed to heaven. Dreams also guided his decision to become a Methodist and his informal attempts at preaching.[109]

On Christmas Day 1787, Asbury noted a dream in his journal in which he prayed for sanctification and says, "God very sensibly filled me with love, and I waked shouting, 'Glory, glory to God!' My soul was all in a flame. I had never felt so much of God in my life."[110]

Dreams and visions figured prominently in the writings of early Methodist people, especially women. Paul Chilcote notes that Dorothy Ripley wrote in her journal, "On 28th 2nd month, 1797, entering my room to worship God, the power of God struck me to the earth, where I lay as covered with his glorious majesty beholding as through His Spirit the riches of His kingdom 'which God hath prepared for them that love him' (1 Cor. 2:9). For some hours I lay on the ground viewing the glory of the city where the Spirit assured me I should dwell forever in bliss unutterable, which then I participated through the overshadowing glory of this visitation which filled me with rapturous joy and surprising awe so that I was lost in wonder, love and praise."[111]

While engaged in prayer and song with some Christian friends, following a discussion of sanctification, Thomas Rankin's "mouth was stopped" and he was "overpowered with the love of God." He said, "I experienced such communion with the Father of spirits, as I never imagined was to be found on this side of eternity." He went on to add, "I did, with Enoch, walk with God! My conversation was indeed in heaven; and I sat with Christ Jesus in heavenly places!"[112]

George White, an African-American who was eventually licensed as a local preacher, and Fanny Newell, a Euro-American woman who preached with her itinerant husband, had the most graphic visions of heaven. White reported, "In the month of May, 1806, at a [class] meeting held in my own house [in New York], I fell prostrate upon the floor, like one dead. But while I lay in this condition, my mind was vigorous and active; and an increasing scene of glory, opened upon my ravished soul; with a spiritual view of the heavenly hosts surrounding the eternal throne, giving glory to God and the Lamb." Fanny Newell, who was "caught up into the third heaven" after a "spark of divine power...took away all [her] bodily strength," said she was "transported by bright Angels...upward to the paradise of God." As she entered "the celestial city," she saw "God and His throne, and...countless armies of shining spirits, who were praising God, and giving glory to the Lamb."[113]

Solomon Shaw notes that "others besides St. Paul have been allowed a view of Paradise, [which] is evident from the testimony of the most reliable witnesses, such as Dr. Tennent, of New Jersey, Dr. Coke, and many others," and he gives an example from James Finley's autobiography:

> One of the most interesting and touching incidents of this character is related by Rev. James B. Finley, in his *Autobiography*. It occurred in 1842, when he was presiding elder of the Lebanon District, Ohio conference. He tells us that he was "winding up the labors of a very toilsome year. I had scarcely finished my work till I was most violently attacked with bilious fever, and it was with great difficulty I reached my home." He sank rapidly. The best medical skill failed to arrest the disease, and life was utterly despaired of. "On the seventh night," he says, "in a state of entire insensibility to all around me, when the last ray of hope had departed, and my weeping family and friends were standing around my couch, waiting to see me breathe my last, it seemed to me that a heavenly visitant entered my room. It came to my side, and in the softest and most silvery tones, which fell like rich music on my ear, it said: 'I have come to conduct you to another state and place of existence.' In an instant I seemed to rise, and gently borne by my angel guide, I floated out upon the ambient air. Soon earth was lost in the distance, and around us on every side were worlds of light and glory. On, on, away, away, from the world to luminous worlds afar, we sped with the velocity of thought. At length we reached the gates of Paradise; and oh, the transporting scenes that fell upon my vision, as the emerald portals, wide and high, rolled back upon their golden hinges!...Language, however, is inadequate to describe what then, with unveiled eyes, I saw.

The vision is indelibly pictured on my heart. Before me, spread out in beauty, was a broad sheet of water, clear as crystal, not a single ripple on its surface, and its purity and clearness indescribable.... At that moment, the power of the eternal God came upon me, and I began to shout and clapping my hands, I sprang from my bed, and was healed as instantly as the lame man in the beautiful porch of the temple, who 'went walking, and leaping, and praising God.' Overwhelmed with the glory I saw and felt, I could not cease praising God."[114]

And then he gives the account of a trance that William Tennent experienced:

In the *Life of William Tennent*, that zealous, devoted minister, and the friend and fellow-laborer of Whitefield, the author or his memoirs gives an account of Tennent being three days in a trance. He became prostrated with a fever, and by degrees sunk under it, until, to appearances, he died. In laying him out, one felt a slight tremor under the left arm, though the body was cold and stiff. The time for the funeral arrived, and the people were assembled. But a physician, Tennent's friend, pled that the funeral might be delayed.... For three days and nights his friend, the physician, never left him. Again the people met to bury him but could not even then obtain the doctor's consent. For more than an hour he pled; when that was gone, he craved half an hour more. That being expired, he implored a stay of fifteen minutes, at the expiration of which Tennent opened his eyes. "As to dying, I found my fever increase, and I became weaker and weaker, until all at once, I found myself in heaven, as I thought.... 'I can say as Paul did, I heard and saw things unutterable.' I saw a great multitude before His glory, apparently in the height of bliss, singing most melodiously. I...was about the join the great and happy multitude, when one came to me, looked me full in the face, laid his hand upon my shoulder, and said: 'You must go back.'...The ravishing sounds of the songs and hallelujahs that I heard, and the very words that were uttered, were not out of my ears, when awake, for at least three years."[115]

Ann Taves writes of trances that were a part of Maria Woodworth's ministry:

> Although not a Methodist, Woodworth identified with the Methodist tradition and was characterized by sympathetic Methodists as promoting "old-fashioned Methodism." ... When people referred to Woodworth as a "trance evangelist," they had both her behavior and that of her followers in mind. Prior to accepting the call to preach, Woodworth experienced visions and at least one out-of-body experience in which she "float[ed] away" from her body and was set down in heaven.... Although from the start "the power" came upon her when she preached, congregations initially responded with more subdued weeping and "death-like solemnity." It was not long, however, before the power of God began to manifest itself in a noisier fashion. At a Methodist church in Ohio in 1882, "all that were present came to the altar and made a full consecration and prayer for a baptism of the Holy Spirit and fire." It came that night, as "fifteen came to the altar screaming for mercy [and] men and women fell and lay like dead." ... This power—manifest in healings, visions, and people falling as if dead—lay at the center of the controversies that surrounded Woodworth revivals.[116]

Taves notes that when children and adults were seized with the power at Trinity M. E. Church in St. Louis, the minister commented "nearly all of them had been at some time or other to the Woodworth meetings, but I do not think that could have had any serious effect, as the doings resembled very much one of the old-fashioned Methodist meetings."[117]

THE WORK OF GOD

Lester Ruth stresses how important the powerful presence of God was for the early Methodists: "The constant desire of early Methodist worship was for God to be present with power to save. They had a standard term for when they thought this occurred: *the work of God.* Methodists used the term to describe the scene within a single service as well as for the outbreak of an extended revival of religion."[118]

For the Methodists, knowing that God was present was not enough. They expected to *feel* God's presence. As Ruth says in another book, "Methodists liked to emphasize *feeling* God's presence...as a physical sensation. One itinerant once noted that the work of God was 'better felt than explained.'...What they felt when the 'work of God' erupted seemed like a Pentecost. And they would use a Pentecost analogy to describe the intensity of God's presence."[119]

Further on Ruth writes, "Early Methodists had a clear goal for their quarterly meetings' preaching services. They prayed for God to be present; they longed for God to be present; they hungered and thirsted for God to be present. In their estimation God often was present, since they could feel the gracious presence in their hearts. They could see the effects of that presence in the variety of reactions in the worshipers: from the first awakenings to God to the joyful, clapping testimonies of those entirely sanctified. Although they honed their skills in preaching and exhorting in fervent hope that God would use their efforts, the 'work of God' often erupted independent of any human effort."[120]

When the power of God would show up, so would physical manifestations. Philip Bruce, presiding elder for the circuits near Norfolk, Virginia, reported that in many places, "as soon as the preacher begins to speak, the power of God appears to be present; which is attended with trembling among the people and falling down; some lie void of motion or breath, others are in strong convulsions: and thus they continue, till the Lord raises them up, which is attended with emotions of joy and rapture." He added, "When one gets happy, it spreads like a flame: so that one after another, they arise to join in the praises of their loving Redeemer."[121]

The Work of God in Class Meetings

Perhaps the most basic group of the Methodist movement was the class meeting. The "work of God" would often be observed in these class meetings.

William Watters presided over a class meeting on the Sussex circuit in Virginia in 1778 when he wrote, "The windows of Heaven were opened, and the Lord poured out such a blessing as our hearts were not able to contain....We were so filled with the love of God, and overawed with His Divine Majesty, that we lay prostrate at His foot-stool, scarcely able to rise from our knees for a considerable time, while there were strong cries and prayers from every part of the house." At a subsequent meeting, "The glorious presence and power of God rested upon us as in a manner I had never known before. For an hour and a half, we all continued constant in prayer and supplication to be saved from sin, that we might be able in our weak manner, while in the world to glorify God, in every breath.... At the class meeting at which Jacob Young was converted many were 'melted into tears,' and fell to the floor 'like trees thrown down by a whirlwind.' 'In a short time,' recalled Young, 'nearly all...were upon the floor, some shouting for joy, others crying aloud for mercy.' Such displays of overt enthusiasm—people crying out or lying slain in the Spirit, unable to stand—were as common in class meetings as at larger public gatherings."[122]

Devereaux Jarratt commented that during the revival, the work of God was especially evident in the "meeting of the classes," and people "flocked to hear, not only me and the traveling preachers, but also the exhorters and [class] leaders." Jarratt added that "whether there was preaching or not, [God's] power was still sensible among the people...at their meetings for prayer."[123]

Richard Garrettson, a local preacher, described how, when the "power came down" in a class meeting and it was no longer possible to speak to the class, the class leaders would open the doors and let everyone in. The noise of the people "induced numbers of people to come, so that in places where we used to have but twenty or thirty on a week day, now there will be a thousand, sometimes more."[124]

The Work of God at Quarterly Meetings

On occasion, Methodists in a region gathered for protracted worship services, lasting several days. The original form of such gatherings was a *quarterly meeting*, which met four times a year for every circuit, usually over a weekend.

Preacher Daniel Asbury wrote a letter to his bishop, describing what happened at one of his quarterly meetings: "On Saturday afternoon, while brother Douthit was at prayer, the mighty power of the Lord came down: many hard-hearted sinners fell to the ground, and cried to the Lord for mercy, as from the belly of hell. The slain of the Lord were many, and numbers that fell, rose again with the new song. The next morning was an awful time: some shouting praise to God, others screaming for mercy, and the whole congregation seemed thunder-struck."[125]

Lester Ruth mentions, writing after an 1802 Kentucky quarterly meeting, that the presiding elder noted, "The Lord was powerfully present; the place was so awful, that the looks of the bystanders visibly proclaimed, 'God is here and we are afraid.'"[126]

The Work of God at Love Feasts

Most Methodists today are unaware of what love feasts were or their significance in early Methodism.

Lester Ruth explains, "A love feast was one of the earliest and most consistent feature of quarterly meetings. They had essentially two parts, the food ritual and the testimonials. The food was bread and water, tokens of Christian fellowship and love. Occasionally, the bread and water were omitted entirely. The food could be omitted but—in the Methodists' estimation—if there were no testimonies (or only 'cold' ones), there was no love feast. The heart of any love feast was its testimonies. These usually occupied the majority of time allotted to a love feast. One Methodist, after hearing the love feast testimonies, became so enamored of Methodism that he considered a sacrifice of 'a thousand worlds' would not have been too great a price to pay for the enjoyment of his religion."[127]

The power of testimony, of hearing how God was moving in people's lives, especially the lives of lay people, was an important part of our Methodist heritage. In the 1960s, the Lay Witness Mission, starting among Methodists, would tap into that same power.

The "work of God" would often break out at love feasts. Concerning one love feast, a participant noted: "It seemed as if the Lord Jesus had come down and visibly stood in the midst of us. The glory of God filled the house." At another love feast, the participant noted that "the power of God [was] manifest in the assembly."[128]

Francis Asbury wrote in his *Journal*, Maryland, Saturday, November 7, 1789, "At Anamessex quarterly meeting, the Lord was among the people on the first day. On Sunday, at the love-feast, the young were greatly filled, and the power of the Most High spread throughout.... There were very uncommon circumstances of a supernatural kind said to be observed at this meeting. The *saints of the world* are dreadfully displeased at this work, which after all, is the best evidence that it is of God."[129]

The Work of God at Holy Communion

Holy Communion was another place where the "work of God" would break out. Lester Ruth points out that the Methodists had a strong awareness of the presence of God at Communion. As one put it, "Our good God was pleased to meet us at His table." At times the intense sensibility of God's presence led Methodists to experience what they called "raptures" or "ecstasies" of joy in the sacrament. The Methodist affirmation that God was present in their sacrament was often connected with a notion of God's power. If God was present, then God was present in power. Other accounts make God's presence synonymous with God's power by noting that during the sacrament, "the power came down." Another wrote, "I administered the Lord's Supper to near 100 precious souls, and the power of the Lord came down in a wonderful manner.... The flame soon increased and spread from heart to heart, and glory be to God! The shout of a King was heard in our Camp." At a quarterly meeting in 1789, the distribution of the bread and wine for Holy Communion was delayed for two hours because the presence of God descended in power upon the gathering.[130]

The Work of God at Camp Meetings

Over time, a longer style of gathering evolved from the quarterly meetings, which came to be called *camp meetings*. Families came to camp meetings with provisions for housing and sustenance that allowed them to stay for a week or more and attend the numerous preaching and prayer services. The highlight of these meetings was when the people would take Holy Communion together. In fact, the meetings themselves were often called "communions."

The most famous of these camp meeting gatherings was the Cane Ridge Revival in Kentucky, of 1800, where between ten thousand to twenty-five thousand people gathered. The largest city in Kentucky at the time, Lexington, only had eighteen hundred citizens at the time, so you can get an idea of the size of this gathering.[131] That revival continued for over a year.

The Cane Ridge Revival featured mainly Presbyterian preachers, but Methodists were there as well. What began as a communion service erupted into what some have called a "frolic of faith." At that revival, one could observe such phenomena as falling, jerking, barking like dogs, falling into trances, the "holy laugh," and "such wild dances as David performed before the Ark of the Lord." One Presbyterian preacher counted three thousand people lying on the ground at one time at Cane Ridge. Another observer reported, "At one time I saw at least five hundred, swept down in a moment as if a battery of a thousand guns had been opened upon them and then immediately followed shrieks and shouts that rent the very heavens."[132] Others would get the "jerks" and shake helplessly in every joint. Methodist circuit rider Peter Cartwright reported that he once saw five hundred jerking at once in one service. The unconverted were as subject to the jerks as were the saints. One minister reported that "the wicked are much more afraid of it than of small pox or yellow fever." After "praying through," some would crawl on all fours and bark like dogs, thus "treeing the devil." Others would fall into trances for hours, awakening to claim salvation or sanctification. In some services entire congregations would be seized by the "holy laugh." It is estimated that by 1805, over half of all the Christians in Kentucky had exhibited these behaviors.[133] Many Methodists would have been included in that number.

Regarding the jerks, an observer at Cane Ridge commented, "Their heads would jerk back suddenly, frequently causing them to yelp or make some other involuntary noise.... Sometimes the head would fly every way so quickly that their features could not be recognized. I have seen their heads fly back and forward so quickly that the hair of females would be made to crack like a carriage whip, but not very loud."[134]

Evidently, the jerks first showed up in Tennessee.[135] It seemed to be contagious. Those who thought it was ridiculous would soon start jerking themselves. A Presbyterian preacher heard that a neighboring congregation was afflicted with the jerks and went to correct them. He started jerking himself, and then when his people gathered to hear his report of the visit, they started jerking. Most convincing was the contagious effect on those who merely visited the camps out of curiosity or to deride. Proud young gentlemen and young ladies, "dressed in their silks, jewelry, and prunella, from top to toe," would turn up, and it amused Cartwright to see them suddenly take the jerks: "The first jerk or so, you would see their fine bonnets, caps, and combs fly, and so sudden would be the jerking of the head that their long loose hair would crack almost as loud as a waggoner's whip."[136]

Second Great Awakening historian Richard McNemar, writing about the history of the revival as a contemporary, wrote of the "dancing exercise," where people would dance under the influence of the Spirit. He told of Brother John Thompson, who was "constrained...for an hour or more to dance in a regular manner round the stand, all the while repeating in a low tone of voice—'This is the Holy Ghost—Glory!'" McNemar also wrote of a heavenly perfume that sometimes filled the air. It was understood to be a sign of God's presence, and under the influence of this perfume "they would swoon away sometimes three or four times in a day, recover, rise and dance around with...incarnate and elevated springs."[137]

Charles Ferguson notes, "An analyst would be hard put to explain the practice of holy barking, unless he speculated that the victim was a reincarnated werewolf. A person would drop to his all fours and run around snapping and growling and making guttural sounds similar to the barking of a dog....A preacher in lower Kentucky reported that 'it was common to see people barking like a flock of spaniels on their way to meeting.' They might remain quiet for a while at meeting and then 'start up suddenly in a fit of barking, rush out, roam around, and in a short time come barking and foaming back.'...It was said to be not uncommon to see numbers of men gathered about a tree, barking, yelping, 'treeing the devil.'"[138]

Barton Stone, the Presbyterian most associated with the Cane Ridge Revival (and forefather of the Disciples of Christ and Churches of Christ and United Church of Christ), reports his own experience with barking in his own memoirs at a time when he was "seized by the jerks." Furthermore, Richard McNemar records people manifesting in a similar way nearly two hundred years ago, when, overwhelmed by God's

Spirit, they "take the position of a canine beast, move about on all fours, growl, snap the teeth, and bark." Edward Scribner Ames, a philosopher with the University of Chicago, wrote in 1910 that in revival meetings, "many strange extravagances—falling, jerking, jumping, rolling, barking—have occurred."[139] (One of the greatest objections from heresy hunters during the Toronto Renewal of the 1990s centered around barking. The times when people barked at Toronto could be counted on one hand. Many more Methodists barked at the camp meetings than the people did at Toronto!)

Vinson Synan, in his book *The Twentieth-Century Pentecostal Explosion*, writes that "the frontier Methodists became famous...for their expressive worship and the demonstrations that often accompanied their revivals. Such exercises as 'the jerks,' 'treeing the devil,' 'being slain in the Spirit,' 'the holy dance,' and 'the holy laugh' were not uncommon in these services. They were often laughingly called 'Methodist fits.' To the faithful, however, they were seen as signs of God's presence and power. Thus, if people fell on the floor, 'slain by the Spirit' while a Methodist preacher ministered, it was considered the best sign that he was called to be a bishop."[140] (Wouldn't that be an interesting criterion to use in our selection of United Methodist bishops today!)

Seeds of the great Cane Ridge camp meeting revival were sown in the nearby town of Red River by a Methodist. The Presbyterian church was sponsoring a series of meetings that proceeded quietly and reverently Friday through Sunday, but on Monday after the service was over, a Methodist preacher, John McGee, who had been invited to the meetings, got up to preach. He exhorted people to let the Lord God omnipotent reign in their hearts and to submit to Him. People began to cry and shout. Someone reminded him that this was a Presbyterian church and that the congregation would not condone such emotionalism. Later John McGee commented, "I turned to go back and was near falling; the power of God was strong upon me. I turned again and, losing sight of the fear of man, I went through the house shouting and exhorting with all possible ecstasy and energy, and the floor was soon covered with the slain."[141]

Mark Galli writes about another of McGee's meetings: "McGee

reported that at Desha's Creek many thousands of people attended. The mighty power and mercy of God was manifested. The people fell before the Word like corn before a storm of wind, and many rose from the dust with divine glory shining in their countenances."[142]

It was to the Red River services that Barton Stone, the Presbyterian pastor of the Cane Ridge church for which the revival was named, came and took the story and the revival back to his people, where it exploded.[143]

Because of the Cane Ridge Revival, the Presbyterians doubled, the Baptists tripled, and the Methodists quadrupled.[144] In Kentucky alone, the Baptist churches added ten thousand members and the Methodists forty thousand.[145]

For almost four decades after 1805, the Methodists were the only denomination to use the camp meeting extensively and regularly. Bishop Francis Asbury promoted them. He urged his preachers to report the camp meetings held in the course of a year. In 1806, the presiding elders of Delaware planned to have one hundred days of camp meetings during the year. They were able to tell the bishop, however, of not one hundred but of one hundred fifty days and nights in the woods and a total of 5,366 converted.[146]

Methodist John Watson criticized the singing at the camp meetings, noting that it had become common for large groups to stay up all night "singing tune after tune, (though with occasional short episodes of prayer) scarce one of which [is] in our hymn books. Some of these, from their nature (having very long repetition choruses and short scraps of matter), are actually composed as sung, and are indeed almost endless."[147] (That sounds like a current frequent criticism of contemporary worship!)

As early as 1807, when Lorenzo Dow returned to England from America with reports of the American camp meetings, British Methodism resisted the fresh move of the Holy Spirit. The British Conference declared, so soon after the days of Mr. Wesley, that open-air preaching to the poor and uneducated was something "highly improper in England." A layman and a local preacher continued to hold open-air revivals in England, and they were expelled from the Methodist Church, precipitating the formation in 1811 of English

Primative Methodism. They sang the American camp meeting songs, and their singing and their antics caused them to be called *ranters*[148] At some of these English Primative Methodist camp meetings, between ten thousand and twenty thousand are said to have been present. Again and again there were scenes of divine demonstration and the power of the Holy Ghost.[149]

From Kentucky, the revivalistic flame spread over the entire South. In most places the same physical phenomena were repeated. In some areas the additional manifestation of speaking in tongues showed up.

In the revival that hit the University of Georgia in 1800–1801, students visited nearby camp meetings and were themselves smitten with the jerks and speaking in tongues: "They swooned away and lay for hours in the straw prepared for those 'smitten of the Lord,' or they started suddenly to flee away and fell prostrate as if shot down by a sniper, or they took suddenly to jerking with apparently every muscle in their body until it seemed they would be torn to pieces or converted into marble, or they shouted and talked in unknown tongues."[150]

The first Methodist camp meeting in the New York City area was held in 1804 and on the Delmarva Peninsula in 1805. Camp meetings under Methodist auspices were not simply associated with the frontier but took place in the established heartlands of Methodism, from New York to Georgia.[151]

For example, James Jenkins wrote regarding a camp meeting on the Bladen circuit near Wilmington, North Carolina, in 1804: "We began the exercises after breakfast, and continued nearly till night, with very little stir; but under the last prayer *the power of God came down* among the people. The saints began to shout aloud and praise God. And sinners began to cry for mercy. In a little time, there were many agonizing on the ground." Thomas Sargent used similar language to describe a camp meeting near Baltimore the same year: "Our strong lunged men exerted themselves until the whole forest echoed, and all the trees of the woods clapped their hands. *God came near,* sinners fell in abundance, Christians rejoiced and shouted, and a glorious sacrifice of praise ascended to God."[152]

By 1811, American Methodists were conducting four hundred to five hundred camp meetings annually. Nathan Hatch has suggested that more than 1 million annually attended Methodist camp meetings by this time.[153]

Most of the new camp meetings were begun by Methodists. The circuit rider and the camp meeting were the two major factors that led the Methodist Church to become the largest Protestant church in America by 1900. Methodism grew from fifteen thousand members in 1784 to slightly less than 1 million in 1830.[154]

The famous circuit rider Peter Cartwright was touched by the Cane Ridge Revival. He wrote in his autobiography, "Many nights, in early times, the itinerant had to camp out, without fire or food for man or beast. Our pocket Bible, Hymn Book, and Discipline constituted our library. It is true we could not, many of us, conjugate a verb or parse a sentence, and murdered the king's English almost every lick. But there was a Divine unction attended the word preached, and thousands fell under the mighty hand of God, and thus the Methodist Episcopal Church was planted firmly in this Western wilderness, and many glorious signs have followed, and will follow, to the end of time."[155]

Rev. James Porter, in his *Compendium of Methodism*, written in 1856, said, "Multitudes of our ministers were converted at camp meetings, and owe their ministerial standing to their influence in reviving and stimulating them to duty. When called to preach, they had their cherished plans of life laid and disliked to abandon them.... But the camp meeting broke the fatal spell. They *heard, felt,* and submitted their whole being to God, and were restored, and endowed for their calling. Many, too, have been sanctified of these occasions."[156]

Camp meetings had their critics. Some objected that they were "nurseries of enthusiasm."[157] Commenting on that, Porter wrote, "There is another kind of enthusiasm which, in our opinion, is most dangerous of all. We refer to a *sleepy* and *inoperative* profession of religion, that does but little for the cause, and that little in a spiritless way. Much as we deprecate wild-fire, we prefer it over no fire at all."[158]

The National Camp Meeting Association

Richard Riss notes that the powerful presence of God continued in camp meetings organized by the National Camp Meeting Association:

The "Pastoral Address" of the Methodist bishops to the 1864 General Conference...decried a loss of spirituality in the church and called for revival. Then, in April of 1865, Methodist Episcopal papers were reporting spiritual awakenings throughout the church. In Indiana there were 11,494 converts within a period of six weeks....In 1867, a group of Methodist Episcopal ministers voted to hold a camp meeting at Vineland, NJ,...naming themselves "The National Camp Meeting Association for the Promotion of Christian Holiness."...The opening of this camp meeting is often considered the beginning of the modern Holiness movement in the United States, since within forty years it resulted in the formation of over a hundred Holiness denominations throughout the world....From the time of this meeting until 1883, a total of 52 "national camps" were held. The second was in the summer of 1868 near Manheim, PA, where, after Dr. G. W. Woodruff began to pray aloud, the following events transpired: All at once, as sudden as if a flash of lightning from the heavens had fallen upon the people, one simultaneous burst of agony and then of glory was heard in all parts of the congregation; and for nearly an hour, the scene beggared all description....Those seated far back in the audience declared that the sensation was as if a strong wind had moved from the stand over the congregation. Several intelligent people, in different parts of the congregation, spoke of the same phenomenon....Sinners stood awestricken, and others fled affrighted from the congregation.[159]

That same year, John Inskip, pastor of the Spring Garden Methodist Episcopal Church in Philadelphia, began conducting "holiness revivals" in the South. At his own church in the fall of 1870, he prayed for the baptism of the Holy Spirit to come upon the congregation and "'in an instant, very many in the audience began to weep.' They all fell upon their knees....In the following year he took a group to California where a witness reported that he saw many prominent leaders of the California conference 'stricken to the ground by the power of God,' and lying for hours, 'filled with the glory.'"[160] (John

Inskip led virtually all the camp and tabernacle meetings sponsored by the National Camp Meeting Association up until his death in 1883.)

Ann Taves tells the story of a dramatic demonstration of the power and presence of God in California: "At a camp meeting in Sacramento it was reported that...a wonderful power came upon all. Many were stricken down under the mighty shock. Many felt themselves beginning to go down as when metal begins to melt, and seemed forced to lie prostrate upon the ground. There was an indescribable power that went surging through the soul, until life seemed suspended on a single thread. It would have been easy then to have taken another step and passed over the narrow stream that separated this from the heavenly land.... Then, also a strange thing occurred to some. It was not a light, nothing of a cloud-form; but as it were, a haze of golden glory encircled the heads of the bowed worshippers—a symbol of the Holy Spirit; for then that company knew that they were baptized with the Holy Ghost and fire. The preachers seemed transfigured. All were melted into tears and sobs, and murmurs of praise and glory. Truly the day of Pentecost has finally come—and the scene of the upper chamber was repeated, and all were filled with the Spirit.... The defining feature of the Methodist camp-meeting tradition was its insistence on the presence of God in the camp and in the individual."[161]

(For another dramatic story of the power of God in a Methodist meeting, see Appendix 3, "A Cyclone of Power and Glory in Answer to Prayer.")

QUENCHING INFLUENCES

By the turn of the century, Methodism was the largest Protestant denomination in America. In 1890, eighty-four of every one thousand Americans were Methodist. And then there was a dramatic decline. Between 1890 and 1990, forty-five thousand Methodist churches were closed. (We have around thirty-seven thousand UM churches left in America today.)

Soon the Spirit would be largely quenched among the Methodists, for several reasons.

First of all, there was the influence of James Buckley, the editor of the preeminent Methodist journal *The Christian Advocate*.

Buckley also wrote a two-volume history of Methodism that high-
lighted the development of its legal and ecclesiastical institutions
and all but ignored Methodism's beginnings as a denomination of
supernatural religious experiences. Buckley became editor of *The
Christian Advocate* in 1880 and retained that position for thirty-two
years. It was during these years that the Faith-Cure movement and
the Pentecostal revival broke out. Buckley vigorously opposed both.
He played a key role in turning the Methodist denomination away
from healing and Pentecostalism at a time when Methodism was a
hair's breadth away from being the first mainline denomination to
embrace both. What the history of American Christianity would
have been like if Methodism had become a Pentecostal denomination in the 1890s can only be imagined. Many Methodists were part
of the Holiness revival and ended up leaving Methodism due to the
direction that Buckley was leading it.[162]

Buckley was opposed to the recovery of the ministry of exorcism
that was being rediscovered by Protestant missionaries on foreign
fields. He wanted to steer the Methodists away from experience-ori-
ented Wesleyan theology and toward Calvinistic cessationism.[163]

Faith healing gained popularity in conjunction with annual "Faith
Conventions" held to promote sanctification (or the second blessing)
at Methodist camp meeting grounds. The convention held at Old
Orchard Beach, Maine, in 1882 attracted widespread note in the
Methodist periodicals. *Zion's Herald,* published by the New England
annual conference, commented on "the great number of testimonies
given of physical healing in answer to prayer." The rapid increase in
such testimonies indicated, according to the editor, that the church
was passing into an era in which "the saints are taking Christ as a
physician of both soul and body."[164]

Buckley gave a caustic assessment of this and published a book crit-
ical of the Protestant faith healing movement. He battled the healing
revival all through the 1880s. He believed that valid spiritual experiences took place only in Bible times and that phenomena like dreams
and visions had naturalistic explanations. He also believed that
turning to healing prayer would produce a Christian who was morally

weakened by the refusal to accept pain and suffering, a flashback to the monastic movement.[165]

The theological arguments that Buckley and others had honed against the gift of healing were easily modified to attack the gift of tongues and other gifts of the Spirit that manifested in the Pentecostal revival of the 1900s.[166]

The second influence that quenched the Spirit was theological liberalism. This movement, stemming from the Enlightenment, said that miracles, signs, and wonders do not happen today and did not happen in the Bible—they are myths or have natural explanations. Theological liberalism took over most of the mainline seminaries.

Laurence Wood notes how quickly this takeover of the seminaries occurred: "The erosion of the Wesleyan doctrinal heritage occurred almost overnight (from 1885 to 1900) when the leadership of the Methodist Episcopal Church changed hands from those committed to its Wesleyan heritage to those who were open to the newer ideas associated with liberal theology imported from Germany and introduced, largely through the writings and teaching of Borden Parker Bowne. This change of Methodist leadership was in some ways more like the overthrowing of the guard than a changing of the guard. Methodist universities in particular self-consciously set aside the tradition conserved from the days of Wesley."[167]

Wood highlights the key influence of Borden Parker Bowne: "In 1876, Bowne began teaching at Boston University, Methodism's oldest center of religious training. Bowne came to have a greater influence on Methodist scholarship than any other thinker. Certainly, his students altered the subsequent course of Methodist thinking, and his method of reconstructing the shape of theology forever changed the way Methodists would do theology. A heresy campaign was waged against Bowne, and a trial was conducted examining his newer theology in 1904. According to the 'Restrictive Rule' adopted in the General Conference of 1808, one could be discontinued as a Methodist preacher if they disagreed with traditional Wesleyan doctrine. Bowne was exonerated, and the doors of Methodism were opened wide to diversity and freedom of theological expression. The ensuing years saw Methodist theological centers of learning largely turn away from traditional Wesleyan doctrine."[168] (That restrictive rule no longer appears in our *Discipline*.)

Riley Case has noted that among the seminaries of all the denominations, Methodists were the first to abandon orthodoxy. When *Minister's Monthly* did a survey of ninety-nine seminaries in 1925 and asked the seminaries to identify their perspectives as orthodox, middle of the road, or liberal, none of the Methodist Episcopal or Methodist Protestant seminaries identified themselves as orthodox and only one identified as middle of the road. The rest saw themselves as liberal. So many Methodist clergy trained in these seminaries began to take on their view of manifestations of the Spirit.[169]

Ann Taves notes, "The religious education movement was a modernist effort to reformulate theological education and parish ministry around a vision of ministry as education....By 1920...rationalistic, developmental psychology...was firmly ensconced in the new departments of religious education in the university-related divinity schools and the more liberal Methodist and Baptist theological seminaries."[170]

Taves continues, "As Arthur McGiffert, president of Union [Theological Seminary] and past president of the Religious Education Association, wrote in 1919, 'Religious education in a democracy should not be such as to encourage the delusive belief in supernatural agencies and dependence upon them, but it should be such to convince everybody that things can be controlled and moulded by the power of man.'"[171]

The new Sunday school curriculum ultimately trivialized the miracles, depicting the early Christians as succumbing to the "common tendency to overemphasize mere marvels....Pentecost did not actually appear as part of the life of Jesus or elsewhere in the graded curriculum....God's presence was not to be sought in unusual experiences or unexpected or extraordinary events."[172]

One can imagine how difficult it was for new ministerial candidates who believed in the supernatural manifestations of the Spirit to face their boards of ordained ministry. If they faced liberals, who did not believe there ever were any true manifestations, the candidate was unacceptable. If they faced conservatives, who were largely cessationists influenced by Buckley, who said there were no manifestations today, the candidate was unacceptable to them as well.

A third quenching influence was John Fanning Watson, a Philadelphia Methodist concerned with middle-class respectability. Lester Ruth points out that Watson "started writing vigorously and systematically against ecstasy in the 1810s.... Over time Watson's viewpoint gained ground. Higher economic levels, increased education for preachers, and a growing desire for social respectability all contributed to diminishing the extent of exuberance and ecstasy among American Methodists. Such spirituality filtered to the margins of the Methodist Episcopal church while remaining stronger, at least initially, in movements and churches branching off from this main trunk."[173]

Watson wrote a book in 1814 that was published anonymously under the title *Methodist Error; or, Friendly Christian Advice to Those Methodists Who Indulge in Extravagant Emotions and Bodily Exercises.* He was not opposed to these things in private devotion but felt these things should not be done in public worship. He marginalized these more "zealous" Methodists by labeling them a minority and marking them in terms of race and class.

Ann Taves notes that in Watson's preface to the "improved edition" of 1819, he reported that Methodism had gone up in the eyes of outsiders as a result of his book, "because they now perceive that the excesses of a few, were never the acts of the whole." The "excesses of the few" were firmly identified with the poor and illiterate, and he took pains to locate the origins of these "errors," "in Virginia, and as I have heard, among the blacks."[174]

Watson, and those who agreed with him, also had their detractors, those who felt that the direction in which he would see the church move would kill the church. Rev. James Porter, in his *Compendium of Methodism* written in 1856, mentions a "general revival of religion" and "the out-pouring of the Spirit of God upon the public heart" from 1840–1844.[175] There was a prediction that Christ would return, and "while few believed the doctrine that Christ would return in 1843, many *feared* it."[176] And many were truly converted in spite of the mistaken teaching. While it is said that the Methodist Episcopal Church suffered a net decrease of more than 50,000 members between the years 1844 and 1847, it should be noted that in 1843, the church's net increase was 154,634; and the year following, 102,831; making a net increase in two years of 257,465 members; thus exceeding all precedent by tens of thousands.[177] Even then, there were those who were "preaching against *excitement* and ridiculing revival measures." And Porter called on others to "abandon their *freezing operations*."[178]

By the mid-1800s, indictments had been widely sounded that Methodism had indeed become too formal, too liberal; that "heart religion" was fading out; and that Wesley's doctrines of entire sanctification and heart purity were being neglected. In response to this, the holiness agitation reached its climax in the latter part of the 1800s, having birthed the National Camp Meeting Association in 1867 and spawned many, many new holiness bodies, thereby fracturing Methodism.[179] Many of these new holiness churches retained the holiness part of Methodism's history but rejected the supernatural part and became cessationist. Following the lead of the Nazarenes, the Wesleyan Methodist Church, the Salvation Army, the Pilgrim Holiness Church, and the Free Methodist Church also disassociated themselves completely from the Pentecostal movement.[180]

Methodism had grown by leaps and bounds in its first one hundred years, especially among the poor and downtrodden. When the Methodist Episcopal Church adopted the first social creed in 1908, it addressed problems of the poor, but at that very time the poor were abandoning Methodism in droves. The poor were not buying into the idea that education and respectability were the future of Methodism.

William Booth, an ordained minister in the Methodist New Connexion body in England, left that pulpit and in 1878 formed the Salvation Army. He wrote, "What I wanted to see was an organization with the salvation of the world as its supreme ambition and object." Specifically concerning tongues, healings and miracles, Booth wrote: "There is not a word in the Bible which proves that we may not have them in the present time....I long for them myself. I believe in their necessity, and I believe they are already among us. The poor infidel world would be made to see all of God that is possible, in order that it may believe."[181]

In Los Angeles, in 1895, the Pentecostal Church of the Nazarene was started by Methodist Phineas Bresee. He wrote of a powerful touch from God that he received:

> I sat alone in the parsonage, in the cool of evening, in the front parlor near the door. The door being opened, I looked up into the azure in earnest prayer, while the shades of evening gathered about. As I waited and waited, and continued in prayer, looking up, it seemed to me as if from the azure there came a meteor, an indescribable ball of condensed light, descending rapidly toward me. As I gazed upon it, it was soon within a few score feet, when I seemed distinctly to hear a voice saying, as my face was upturned towards it: "Swallow it; swallow it," and in an instant it fell upon my lips and face. I attempted to obey the injunction. It seemed to me, however, that I swallowed only a little of it, although it felt like fire on my lips, and the burning sensation did not leave them for several days. While all of this of itself would be nothing there came with it into my heart and being, a transformed condition of life and blessing and unction and glory, which I had never known before. I felt like my need was supplied. I was always very reticent in reference to my own personal experience. I have never gotten over it, and I have said very little relative to this; but there came into my ministry a new element of spiritual life and power. People began to come into the blessing of full salvation; there were more persons converted; and the last year of my ministry in that church was more consecutively successful, being crowned by an almost constant revival. When the third year came to a close, the church had been nearly doubled in membership and in every way built up.[182]

In spite of the supernatural experiences of Booth and Bresee, and the crying out for a new visitation of God by their followers, the denominations that developed from them rejected speaking in tongues and the Pentecostal message. The term "Pentecostal" was removed from the name of the Pentecostal Church of the Nazarene, and it became the Church of the Nazarene.

Chapter Three

MANIFESTATIONS OF THE SPIRIT AMONG METHODIST MISSIONARIES, CENTRAL CONFERENCES, AND AUTONOMOUS METHODIST CHURCHES

R AMSAY MACMULLEN, EMERITUS professor of history and classics at Yale University, set out to find the answer to the question, "How did the early Christians who had no money, no institutions, little education, and whose religion was illegal, conquer the other gods of the Greco-Roman pantheon? How did Christianity become the official religion of the Roman empire in three hundred years?" His research as a secular historian resulted in quite a surprise. The church's success was not primarily due to great preaching or convincing apologetics but to healings and demonic deliverances performed in Jesus' name.[1]

In the two-third's majority world today, which is now the global center of Christendom, miracles are largely more accepted and expected than in the West. Dr. Craig Keener, professor of New Testament at Asbury Theological Seminary, has written a two-volume work titled *Miracles: The Credibility of the New Testament Accounts*, in which he writes:

> Whereas fewer than 18 percent of Christians in 1900 lived outside Europe and North America, today more than 60 percent do, and an estimated 70 percent will by 2025. As the center of world Christianity has shifted to the Global South, the dominant Christian perspectives in the world have shifted with it....Not surprisingly, readings of Scripture in the Global South often contrast starkly with modern Western critics'

readings. These readings from other social locations often shock Westerners not only because others believe the early Christian miracle narratives to be plausible but also because these readers often take these narratives as a model for their ministries.

Thus Western scholar of global Christianity Philip Jenkins notes that, in general, Christianity in the Global South is quite interested in the "immediate workings of the supernatural, through prophecy, visions, ecstatic utterances, and healing." Such an approach, closer to the early Christian worldview than the modern Western culture is, appeals to many traditional non-Western cultures.[2]

Keener goes on to say:

> The majority of Catholics, Pentecostals, Anglicans, and members of most other groups of Christians now live in the Global South, that is, in the majority world; by 2050, perhaps only 20 percent of Christians in the world will be white. Thus, in contrast to the period when many of the plausibility structures (what intuitively strikes us as rational) for modern critical New Testament scholarship were defined, two-thirds-world Christians are now the majority, and expectation of healings is common among many of their churches. "Signs and wonders" are among the most prominent factors drawing people to faith in Christ in the majority world today, with healings and exorcisms proving particularly effective. Dramatic miracle reports tend to cluster in different regions at different times, sometimes during periods that some scholars call "revival"...; as a general rule, however, we may say that these claims are far more common in many regions of Africa, Asia, and Latin America today than in the West.[3]

Keener's own sister-in-law, who is from the Congo, was raised from the dead—an example cited in his book.

Many preachers have preached on the text Acts 1:8, "You will receive power when the Holy Spirit comes on you; and you will be my witnesses in Jerusalem, and in all Judea and Samaria, and to the ends of the earth," as a promise that we would receive power to witness. If you look at the punctuation and language of that verse, Jesus is saying that we will receive power, and the fact that we have received power will witness all over the earth. Christians would display the power of God, and that would witness to the people that the kingdom of God had come, that there was hope of overcoming the life situations they found themselves in. One of the reasons why people turned to Methodism in the past and in mission situations was the power of God they saw displayed among the Methodists.

Missions is at the heart of Methodism. John Wesley went as a missionary to the Native Americans in Georgia (though his efforts were a dismal failure, devoid of the supernatural power displayed later in his ministry in England). Wesley sent preachers as missionaries to America, and we have already seen manifestations of the power of the Holy Spirit in their ministries. But there were other Methodist missionaries who also displayed and experienced this power.

AMONG THE WYANDOT INDIANS

James B. Finley (1781–1856) was converted at Cane Ridge and became a Methodist circuit rider. He worked among the Wyandot Indians of Ohio. He described an 1828 camp meeting among them: "After singing one of their Christian songs, only as Indians can sing, they fell simultaneously upon their knees and lifted up their faces toward heaven. While they were praying the Spirit came down upon them, and the power of God was manifested in the awakening and conversion of souls. The tears and groans and shouts [were] a sign that the Great Spirit was at work upon the hearts of these sons and daughters of the forest. The whole encampment was in a flame of religious excitement, the Lord having taken His own work into His own hands."[4]

INDIA

The Pentecostal revival spread to Methodists around the world. Minnie Adams went to Bombay, India, as a missionary in 1887, where she established a school for orphan girls. One night at the school, one of the girls claimed to be baptized with the Holy Spirit and with fire. Visible tongues of fire appeared on the girl, and someone ran to get a pail of water and was about to douse her with it when they discovered it was not physical fire. That same phenomenon of visible tongues of fire began to happen elsewhere in India, and Minnie wrote her popular book *Baptism of the Holy Ghost and Fire* to urge Christians to pray for the fullness of the Spirit to purify and empower them for mission.[5]

Solomon Shaw tells the story of A. E. Winter. Winter was a missionary of the Methodist Episcopal Church in India. In January 1888, he was appointed by Bishop Thoburn to open work in a district of the native state of Hyderabad, India. The parish embraced more than a thousand towns and villages, of over a million souls—a district practically untouched by Christian evangelism. He visited the village of Kinnal, with probably twelve thousand residents, all Hindu, and began to preach the gospel. The village was stricken with cholera and smallpox, and the people had sacrificed nearly all their poultry, sheep, goats, and much fruit to appease the anger of their gods, and still the scourge went on. For eight months, there had been no rain.

After the message, a man came up and said, "My wife is dying. For days I have been breaking cocoanuts and making poojahs, and my wife has been growing worse all the time; now I beg of you to pray to your God, to see if he will hear and save my wife." Winter and his wife went to see the woman, and she was on the verge of death. He said to the man, "Jesus Christ, who is the only God, can save your wife if He thinks best. Now if He cures her, will you then forever renounce your idols and worship Jesus Christ only?" The man's aged mother rushed up to him in tears and pled with her son to not do this.

The man replied, "I can make better answer after she is cured." But Winter insisted that he could not feel justified in asking his Savior to interfere on the man's behalf unless he was willing to worship Jesus if He showed Himself by His superior power to be God. All the man's relatives and the priests gathered around him and tried to persuade him that it would be better for his wife to die than that he should make such a promise.

Finally, the man said, "Yes, if Jesus Christ can save my wife, it shows that what you say is right—my gods are false and I ought then to worship Jesus Christ." Winter and his wife prayed that the Lord would demonstrate His power among these people by healing this lady. They walked away, and the excited man came running after them yelling, "Jesus Christ, He is God! My wife is well!" Till nearly midnight, the voice of that joyful man was heard going up and down the narrow streets of the village crying out, "Jesus Christ, He is the only true God!" And toward the morning a substantial shower of rain fell and the people said, "It is because the missionary is praying."[6]

In 1905, the Methodist work in India experienced a "Jubilee Revival," which began among Bengali girls and boys in Asansol in north India, and it was accompanied by speaking in tongues. This was an outgrowth of the Great Indian Revival of 1905–1907.[7]

John F. Goucher, an influential Methodist Episcopal Church minister from Baltimore, observed during a tour of India in 1912, "I heard more about the Holy Spirit in the time I was in India [it was a visit of a few months] than in thirty years from the preaching here in America."[8]

CHILE

The Hoovers were Methodist missionaries to Chile at the turn of the century. As they read their friend Minnie Adams' eyewitness account of the remarkable outpouring of the Spirit in India in her book *Baptism of the Holy Ghost and Fire,* they were stirred to pray for a similar revival in Chile. On July 4, 1909, they reported:

> Saturday night was an all night of prayer, during which four vain young ladies (three of them were in the choir) fell to the floor under the power of the Spirit. The following morning in Sunday school…a daze seemed to rest upon the people. Some were unable to rise after the opening prayer which had been like "the sound of many waters," and all were filled with wonder. From that time on the atmosphere seemed charged by the Holy Spirit and people fell on the floor, or broke out in other tongues, or singing in the Spirit. On one occasion a woman, a young lady, and a girl of twelve were lying on the floor in different parts of the prayer room, with eyes closed and silent. Suddenly, as with one voice, they burst forth into a song in a familiar tune but in unknown tongues, all speaking the same words. After a verse or two they became silent; then

again suddenly, another tune, a verse or two, and silence. This
was repeated until they had sung ten tunes, always using the
same word, and keeping in perfect time together as if led by
some invisible chorister.[9]

Vinson Synan notes that after two months, attendance jumped
from three hundred to nearly one thousand. A mission official in New
York City depicted the reports as having "much to compare with the
history of the Methodist revival in its primitive times."[10]

Eddie Hyatt tells about the repercussions from this outpouring:
"Nevertheless, in February 1910, Hoover was forced by his Methodist
superiors to choose between returning to America or leaving the
Methodist Church if he were to remain a missionary in Chile. He
chose to leave the Methodist Church and remain. C. Peter Wagner
has commented, 'Many Methodists who blamed the devil for what
happened in 1909 have since wondered out loud on whose side the
devil might really have been.'"[11] The Pentecostal Methodist Church
in Chile now numbers over 1.5 million members, while the Chilean
Methodist Church has shrunk to four thousand members.[12]

The Jotabeche Pentecostal Methodist Church in the capital of
Santiago has grown to over 100,000 members. At one point it was the
largest Protestant church in the world. With Pentecostals comprising
nearly 15 percent of Chile's population, Chile can be considered the
most Pentecostal nation in the world.[13]

NORWAY, ENGLAND, GERMANY, SWEDEN

Richard Riss writes about Thomas B. Barratt of Norway. Barratt was
a minister of the Methodist Episcopal church who came to America
in 1906 to raise money for missions in Norway. While there, he heard
the reports coming from the Azuza Street Revival in Los Angeles,
and he began to seek the baptism of the Holy Spirit. In 1907, he testified that he spoke and sang by the power of the Spirit in several different languages. A supernatural light was seen like a cloven tongue of
fire over his head.[14] He returned to Norway and began to preach his
new Pentecostal message. People in Norway then began to speak in
tongues, and tongues of fire were seen over Barratt's head in Norway.

Alexander Boddy, Anglican rector from Sunderland, England,

visited Barratt's meetings in Oslo. Through Boddy, the Pentecostal revival spread throughout England. Jonathan Paul, a leader in the Holiness Movement in Germany, was also baptized in the Holy Spirit through Barrett's meetings in Oslo,[15] as was Lewi Prethus, a young Swedish Baptist pastor who then was one of the instruments of taking the Pentecostal revival to Sweden.[16]

In February 2012, Kevin Basconi came and ministered at the fourth session of the Methodist School for Supernatural Ministry at the Aldersgate Renewal Center in Goodlettsville, Tennessee (www.kingof-gloryministries.com). In July 2012, Kevin ministered in St. Peter's United Methodist Church in Stockholm, Sweden, and the power of God broke out in healings and creative miracles.

MEXICO

In the 1920s, Francisco Olazabel was a Mexican trained Methodist minister who criticized and persecuted Pentecostals. Then he was baptized in the Holy Spirit at a prayer meeting with some missionaries connected with the Assemblies of God, and he left the Methodist Church and was credentialed with the Assemblies of God.[17]

In 1922, Andres Ornelas was a converted Mexican miner who was baptized by a Methodist missionary who introduced him to the doctrine of the baptism in the Holy Spirit and helped him found a Pentecostal church.[18]

KOREA AND CHINA

Luther Oconer notes that Methodism's quest for real Christianity and its consequent holiness and Holy Spirit–themed revivalism would figure prominently within both the Methodist Episcopal Church and Methodist Episcopal Church South mission in Korea through the interdenominational "Korean Revival" in Pyongyang in 1907 and in the Methodist Episcopal Church mission during the "Hinghwa Pentecost" in Hinghwa (now Putian) and in Fookien (now Fujian), China, in 1909–1913. It was during the revival that the young John Sung was converted. Later to become the evangelist of the Hinghwa Conference of the Methodist Church in China, Sung led spectacular

Pentecostal-type revivals in China and among the Chinese diaspora in Taiwan and Southeast Asia in the 1930s.[19]

Methodist evangelist Yong Do Lee began a ministry distinguished by speaking in tongues and healings in Korea in 1928.[20]

Randy Clark comments on revival today in Korea: "One of the greatest revivals in the last hundred years has occurred in the nation of South Korea....One of the unique aspects of the revival in Korea has been that the mainline denominations have been profoundly influenced by the charismatic movement. It is common to enter a Methodist or Presbyterian church and find people prophesying, healing the sick, and performing miracles. It is no coincidence that both the largest Methodist church and the largest Presbyterian church in the world are in Korea."[21]

MALAYSIA

In the September 11, 2010, issue of *Christianity Today*, Bishop Hwa Yung of the Methodist Church of Malaysia wrote of his journey from modern education to supernatural Christianity as a result of a careful reading of the Bible and the weight of empirical evidence: "Most liberals denied the supernatural both in the Bible and in the present: Evangelicals fought tooth and nail to defend the miraculous in the Bible, but rarely could cope with it in real life."

He went on to write, "Western Christians often fail to fit the 'signs and wonders' of the Holy Spirit into their theological framework. Up until recently, they have treated classic Pentecostalism as some form of aberrant religion, along with various versions of non-Western indigenous Christianity that also take the New Testament teaching on spiritual gifts and miracles seriously. But today, with Pentecostalism and the Charismatic movement increasingly accepted in the West, and most of the dynamic non-Western churches taking the miraculous seriously, it increasingly looks as if the real aberration is 'mainline' Western Christianity.

"A 21st-century reformation will demand reinserting the supernatural into the heart of Christianity. This will result not only in a sounder biblical theology but also a more powerful missional church. The world will then understand what Jesus means when he said, 'But if it is by the Spirit of God that I cast out demons, then the kingdom of God has come upon you' (Matt. 12:28, ESV)."[22]

In November 1984, the Methodist Church of Malaysia approved a document titled "The Methodist Church and the Charismatic Movement," which made much use of resource material already available, especially from the British Methodist Church and United Methodist Church.

When "Guidelines: The United Methodist Church and the Charismatic Movement" was up for revision and renewal at the 2008 General Conference of the United Methodist Church, an updated draft of the Malaysian Methodist Church document was consulted in the revision that was approved by that General Conference. The draft document of the Methodist Church of Malaysia appears in Appendix 4. The approved United Methodist Church guidelines appear in Appendix 5.

THE PHILIPPINES

Luther Oconer tells the story of the moves of the Holy Spirit among Methodists in the Philippines in his doctoral dissertation. Methodism came to the Philippines from India. Emphasis on the work of the Holy Spirit permeated the Methodist mission in India. Methodism arrived on Philippine shores in 1899. By 1905, the *Advocate* in the Philippines was keeping missionaries abreast of the Welsh Revival, as well as of the spreading revival in India and hopes that a "revival may come to Manila and the Philippines in all its power."[23]

As Dr. Oconer puts it, the holiness revival in the Philippines was set on a "supernaturalistic trajectory."[24]

Lester Sumrall, an Assemblies of God pastor, left his large church in South Bend, Indiana, and arrived in the Philippines with his family in 1952. He conducted salvation and healing crusades and started the Manila Bethel Temple. Sumrall, Oral Roberts, and other healing evangelists were part of a healing revival movement that lasted from 1947–1958, and they infused the standard revival themes of salvation and holiness in Christ with the message of divine healing.[25]

At that time, Ruben Candeleria was the district superintendent of the Manila district of the Methodist Church. He saw a longtime acquaintance who was a cripple walking without her crutches after a healing revival sponsored by Sumrall. And he read in the *Manila Times* of the deliverance of a prisoner from demon possession by Sumrall. These two events led Candeleria to yearn for Pentecostal power in his ministry. He met with Sumrall, and Sumrall laid his hands on Candeleria and prayed for him. This started a friendship between the two men.

That friendship paved the way for the official entry of the healing revival among Methodists in the Manila district. Sumrall and Candeleria took Oral Roberts' healing film, *Venture Into Faith,* and spoke in fifty-one churches, mostly Methodist, showing the film, preaching deliverance, and praying for the sick. The campaign culminated during the Manila District Conference held at the Taytay Methodist Church in January 1954, where Sumrall preached to a crowd of about three thousand and prayed for the sick.

The pastor of the Taytay church was Candeleria's first cousin, David Candelaria. David opened his church for a healing revival, and while the Oral Roberts' film was being shown, David was healed of a lingering illness. His wife and eldest son also testified to being healed. That meeting thrust the Taytay church not only to the forefront of the Manila healing revival, but also on a trajectory toward Pentecostalism.

Despite the positive results of the salvation-healing campaign in Methodist churches, the Methodist leadership was unhappy with the collaboration between Sumrall and the Candelerias. This came to a head at the annual conference of 1954, and Ruben filed for "voluntary withdrawal" at the 1955 conference. It was in that same year that he claimed to have experienced the baptism of the Holy Spirit "according to the Bible pattern." After four days of fasting, he spoke in "another tongue" for an hour and a half after being prayed for by the two in his office.

Four days later, Ruben's cousin, David, also experienced his "Pentecostal infilling." About a week after that experience, David hosted a weeklong revival meeting in his Taytay Methodist church. The first evening, an outpouring of the Holy Spirit came to the church, which a church member said was "similar to Acts 2." David and other witnesses also claimed that a large cloud of smoke billowed from the church building, which prompted about two hundred people to rush to the church, some even carrying buckets of water to douse the fire. When they arrived, what they found instead, according to David, was the "fire of the Holy Spirit." About eighty people spoke in tongues for the first time while most of them lay "slain on the floor."

This experience of the Taytay congregation strained their relationship with the Methodist Church. When the bishop wanted to transfer David to another church, he decided to leave and form his own congregation. Less than half of the congregation remained with the Methodist church under the new pastor. This Pentecostal impulse never left the Taytay United Methodist congregation completely, as it experienced a resurgence in the 1980s and early '90s with the growth of the charismatic movement in the country. The church, which remains charismatic in orientation to this day, emerged as the fastest-growing United Methodist congregation in the Philippines during that period. Prominent Taytay Methodists were also instrumental in the forming of the Aldersgate United Methodist Renewal Fellowship in the Philippines.[26]

In 1992, a group of United Methodist ministers, laypersons, and then Bishop Solito K. Toquero launched the Aldersgate United Methodist Renewal Fellowship, the only charismatic renewal movement in a Philippine Protestant mainline denomination today. The movement attracts more than one thousand Filipino United Methodists to its annual Aldersgate Conference, held the first week in January in Baguio City. The formation of the Aldersgate movement led Bishop Emerito P. Nacpil of the Manila Episcopal Area to issue a circular, dated August 19, 1993, to "not oppose the charismatic movement within our United Methodist constituency."[27] All of the United Methodist bishops in the Philippines have attended the most recent Aldersgate conferences in that country.

PARAGUAY

The New Horizon School is an advance special project of the United Methodist Church in Paraguay. The missionary director of the school, Sue Givens, reports that the children began to pray for the sick with miraculous results happening. Julio, a student there, was diagnosed with leukemia. He was told that he would have to have chemo that would cause him to vomit and lose all his hair. Julio said this would not happen, that God would take care of him. He did not vomit and did not lose any hair. He is playing soccer again.

When in eighth grade, Juan's mother was suffering with terrible leg pains. He said, "Mom, let me pray for you." He put his hand on his mom's leg and began praying. The whole family was watching, and the older ones were snickering. Within a few minutes, his mother's leg pains were completely gone.

The director's mother had a fast-growing tumor that doctors said would kill her if it was not removed. Due to other medical conditions, there was only a 50 percent chance that she would survive surgery. The school and church prayed for her, and one night at a very powerful, Spirit-filled service, the pastor told the director, "Your mother has just been healed." Several days later, the mother called and said, "It is gone!" The doctors could not find any sign of the mass or tumors. (For more information on the New Horizon Methodist School, see www.paraguayschools.org.)

NEW ZEALAND

Craig Marsh was a dying man from New Zealand who came to a United Methodist pastor's conference in Florida. His wife kissed him goodbye in New Zealand and sent a friend with him to bring his body back, since he was not expected to survive the trip. He had terminal cancer and had his entire stomach and part of his intestines removed. At that United Methodist pastor's meeting, God totally removed the cancer and created a brand-new stomach where there was none before. Now God has sent him on a worldwide healing ministry, and he ministers in quite a number of UMC churches. (For more information on Craig Marsh, see www.turningpointministries.info.)

TOGO

Dr. Vince Brawley, member of Trinity on the Hill UMC in Augusta, Georgia, went on a short-term medical mission trip to Baga village, Togo, West Africa, to work with Mission Society missionaries there. While there, he examined a woman named Bernadette, whom he diagnosed with advanced, untreatable, metastatic breast cancer. She had only months or maybe weeks to live. He and others laid hands on her and prayed, but having little faith in her healing made preparations for the support of her three young children after her death.

The Mission Society missionaries had been holding a Bible study in Bernadette's home, and they continued to pray for her. During this time, they sensed her faith was growing and getting stronger. She was enjoying feeling the presence of the Lord in her. The missionaries came back to the US for a time and then returned to Togo. Dr. Brawley asked them about Bernadette. They reported that they had visited Bernadette's home and she appeared from her hut and fell at the missionaries' feet, proclaiming the mighty power of God. She was completely healed! No more tumors, one of which was the size of a grapefruit and the other the size of an orange. There were just some scars where there had been ulcerating sores before.[28]

NEPAL

In 2009, I led an Aldersgate Renewal Ministries team to Nepal to hold a Life in the Spirit seminar and Lord, Teach Us to Pray seminar for United Methodists there. I was told that the United Methodist Church is growing rapidly in Nepal because ordinary Nepali United Methodist laypeople go into their villages and heal the sick and cast out demons. When the Hindu and Buddhist Nepalis encounter a God of power who delivers them from their sickness and demonization, they renounce their former gods and turn to the powerful God of the United Methodists. A study revealed that about 34 percent of those who came to Christ in Nepal did so because of a healing.

The presence of the Holy Spirit was powerful during the seminars. After a presentation on the baptism in the Holy Spirit, prayer was offered over the people, asking the Spirit to come down upon the participants as at Pentecost, and some of the people began to shake, others began to weep, still others cried out to God. It was very much like early Methodist meetings!

A man who had been paralyzed testified that the United Methodists came and prayed for him, he was healed, and he left Hinduism to follow Christ. A former Hindu priest and former idol carver both testified to coming to Christ because of the United Methodists. A mother whose daughter suffered from epilepsy said that the United Methodists prayed for her daughter and she was healed, so the mother gave her life to Christ. Another woman whose son was mentally ill was prayed for by the United Methodists and healed, so she gave her life to Christ as well.

LIBERIA

In 2010, I led an Aldersgate Renewal Ministries team to hold a Life in the Spirit seminar at the United Methodist Gbarnga School of Theology. While there I was told that as people are baptized in United Methodist Church services in Liberia, they often manifest demons acquired in their past life, and the pastors minister deliverance to them before they can continue on their journey of Christian discipleship.

FIJI

When John Hunt began preaching holiness in Viwa, Fiji, in 1845, a revival broke out among many converts who, in Hunt's words, had been previously "careless and useless." Spontaneous emotional outbursts and physical manifestations accompanied the revival so that business on the island was suspended for several days.[29]

The Sentinel Group, in the 2004 documentary *Let the Sea Resound,* covers an astonishing revival sweeping through the nation of Fiji at that time. They highlight the unprecedented Christian unity, contemporary signs and wonders, rapid church growth, and sociopolitical transformation. Even the land and the sea were revived by the breath of God. In their coverage, the involvement of the Methodist Church in that revival is clear. It is the largest Christian denomination in Fiji. (For more information see www.revivalworks.com and www.sentinelgroup.org.)

Today the operations of the Methodist Church are being restricted by the government there.

CUBA

Larry Davies tells the story of the moving of the Holy Spirit among Methodists in Cuba. Bishop Pereira of the Methodist Church of

Cuba has been the bishop there for over 15 years. During that time, the Methodist Church went from the verge of extinction (because of Castro and Communist harassment) to a church that is now thriving with hundreds of new churches growing rapidly throughout Cuba. What a miracle. But how did it happen?

Bishop Pereira tells of a woman he met shortly after becoming a bishop. She introduced herself as a Communist official and immediately started poking her finger in his chest while promising that within five years, his churches would all be gone. Several years later, he noticed her in the front row of one of his churches at a worship service. She stood up and gave her testimony about how God changed her life through the Methodist Church.

In 1975, there were very few Methodist churches or Methodists in Cuba, possibly less than five hundred people. In 2000, there were 136 churches and just over ten thousand Methodists. Today there are 361 churches and more than thirty thousand Methodists.

Many people come to the bishop now and ask to become a pastor. His answer is always the same: "Go and start a church, and then we can talk about you being a pastor." Bishop Pereira says, "They do it. They start a church, and then they come back and ask what to do next?"

There are only a few church buildings allowed in Communist Cuba, so churches are formed in homes, in fields, or wherever Methodists can meet. The bishop smiled as he said this and added, "But make no mistake. They are churches. They have Sunday school, they study the Bible, they worship with intensity, and lives are being changed by Jesus Christ every day."

A video of their last Annual Conference showed an interruption by someone who needed healing. They stopped the proceedings and immediately had a mass healing service.

Bishop Pereira's point is that in the United States, we are way too attached to our buildings, and we often miss opportunities to be the church that is offered by the movement of the Holy Spirit. Every church in America should have several people who want to be pastors who could be starting churches within churches. They do not need buildings. They need encouragement and guidance through the power of the Holy Spirit.

If we are being the church within our community, people should be coming to our pastors and leaders and asking how they can do more to serve our Lord, Jesus Christ. We should respond by saying, "Invite people to your home. Form a Bible study or a prayer group."

At the end of the service, Bishop Pereira said, "God can and will do miracles within our churches, but we must do our part."[30]

The Methodists in Cuba are more Pentecostal than the Pentecostal churches in the United States. Eighty percent of the Methodists in Cuba are Pentecostal in experience.[31]

BRAZIL

The Methodist Church of Brazil has been an autonomous Methodist Church since 1930. Bishop João Carlos Lopes is president of the Council of Bishops there and bishop of the sixth region, headquartered in Curitiba. He teaches his pastors to heal and to prophesy. He expects supernatural ministry to occur in his churches. When pastors graduate from seminary and come to him for a church, he tells them, "No, I am not going to give you a church. You are to give me a church!" He expects his new pastors to be church planters.

American United Methodist evangelist Rick Bonfim takes ministry teams to do supernatural ministry in Brazil several times a year (www.latterain.com). Aldersgate Renewal Ministries led several Life in the Spirit seminars in Brazil with the assistance of Rick Bonfim.

In June 2007, while Rick was ministering in a small Methodist church in one of the most dangerous *favelas* (slums) in the city of Rio de Janeiro, he heard a word from the Lord to send them into the streets and bring in the lost. When he delivered that word, the American students with him and the entire congregation emptied the church in less than five seconds. Soon dozens of young people, many of them armed with guns, began to come into the church and kneel before the cross in the altar area. As they prayed for those that the Lord brought in, Rick testifies, "The air was filled with a mist that covered us all. All I could see was a white glare, as if glory was shining everywhere."

United Methodists Nic and Rachael Billman and Luke and Alisan

Billman have a ministry in Brazil called Shores of Grace. There they teach people to do supernatural ministry on the streets among drug addicts, homosexuals, transvestites, and prostitutes. The Billmans are opening rescue homes to take in children trapped in sex trafficking. (For more information, see www.shoresofgrace.com.)

Aldersgate Renewal Ministries is in the process of assembling a Brazil Power Team, made up largely of senior high youth and young adults (as well as some students from the Methodist School of Supernatural Ministry) who will minister supernaturally with Brazilian Methodists in Brazilian Methodist churches in 2013.

GHANA

The following story from Ghana was shared in a Mission Society news-letter. A young man named John, whose last name has been withheld because he is working toward becoming a Mission Society missionary in a sensitive area, writes this of his experience among the Methodists in Ghana:

> In January of 2009, I hopped on a plane and flew to Ghana, West Africa. I worked in an orphanage and AIDS clinic with the Methodist Church Ghana. It was the most profound experience of my life. I spent time teaching English to about fifteen orphan kids. I loved those kids. The missionaries who I lived with at the time connected me with a Ghanaian pastor. He was a rock star. About seventy-four years old, he still rode his motorcycle into the bush [remote areas] to tell people about Jesus. He took me under his wing, and he shared his life with me.
>
> One day, we went on an evangelistic campaign in a village in the north of Ghana. The missionary I was living with and some Ghanaian pastors set up a projector and showed the *Jesus* film. Once the film was over, a man walked up to us and said, "I saw the movie, and I saw Jesus heal a deaf man." And we said, "Yes, Jesus heals deaf people." He said, "Well, my son has been deaf and mute since birth. Can Jesus heal him?" At this point, I just wanted to hide in the corner. All the Ghanaians were saying, "Yes, God can heal your son. Bring him by tomorrow morning, and we'll pray for him."

And so, on Saturday morning, we had a healing and deliverance service. It was fascinating, but I was totally out of my comfort zone. People started praying in many different languages and in other tongues. I stood in the back taking in all this, but I was skeptical. I have always been a skeptic. I have my doubts about pretty much everything, but the Lord has always proved faithful.

At the end of this time, a man named Ongala was brought to the front by his father. Ongala was about twenty-seven years old. He has been deaf and mute since birth. We started to pray.

I immediately thought of the paralytic in Mark. When his friends couldn't get him to Jesus, they cut a hole in the roof and let him down through it. Jesus looked at them and said, "I say to you, 'Your sins are forgiven.'" And then the Pharisees got angry and asked, "Who are you to forgive sins?" And Jesus said, "Which one is easier? Is it easier to say, 'Your sins are forgiven,' or is it easier to say to this man, 'Take your mat and walk?'" And Jesus said, "So that you may know that the Son of Man has authority on earth to forgive sins, I say to you, 'Rise. Take up your mat and go home.'"

Many of these Ghanaian villagers had just had their first exposure to Jesus. So as we all prayed, my prayer was, "God, if You care whether or not these people know that You have authority to forgive sins, You have to heal this person."

I don't know how to pray for healing, but God showed up. After what seemed like forever, as we prayed for this man, all of a sudden he started to cry. His tongue wasn't completely loose, but he started to make noise for the first time in his life. He started saying, "Yesu," which is the word for *Jesus* in his language. My mind was blown. I don't know why. Jesus meant what He said. And what He said was true. So why should I be surprised that He is able to heal a deaf person? He did it in the Bible a number of times.

God just really struck me that I needed to have more faith. I needed to believe in the promises of God, and I needed to believe that what God said was true and actually live it out in a more profound way.[32]

PERU

Martin Reeves is an elder in the New Mexico annual conference serving with the Mission Society in Peru. The parents of six children, Martin and Tracy were anticipating the arrival of another daughter, Jubilee Faith. Tracy had miscarried three times during the course of several years, so she and Martin were thrilled when they learned she was pregnant again. An ultrasound, though, revealed that the baby had a hole in her heart.

Within a week of learning of their baby's condition, Martin traveled to Huancayo for missionary training of nationals. While praying with the men in his training group, he had a vision that he needed to get home and place his hands on Tracy for their new baby, Jubilee. After the group prayer, when the men said, "Amen," the leader of the team said to Martin, "I just had this vision of you placing your hands on your wife's stomach, and I saw this light passing through her back and just bursting forth through the womb!"

When Martin arrived home, he placed his hands on Tracy's stomach, just as in his vision, and they prayed for the healing of baby Jubilee. Within days, after reviewing a new ultrasound, the doctor told Tracy and Martin, "I can't find the hole here; it's not there! This never happens in the womb. Sometimes after birth, the hole will close by itself, but I've never seen this happen in the womb!" Martin told the doctor, "We serve an awesome and powerful God, a God who is still active and interested in us, and He knows our desires and our needs."

God used the birth of healthy Jubilee Faith to heal the hearts of Martin and Tracy and their six other children. "Because of the miscarriages, our youngest children remembered the hospital only as a place where babies went to heaven," says Tracy. "Jubilee Faith's birth helped heal all of our wounds."

Martin says, "Our oldest son held Jubilee Faith in his arms and just began to cry, saying, 'Wow, what a tremendous blessing.' She is our precious miracle from God."[33]

ARM INTERNATIONAL MINISTRIES

Aldersgate Renewal Ministries (ARM) shares Wesley's passion for ministry to the world. On June 11, 1739, John Wesley wrote in his

Journal: "I look on all the world as my parish; thus far I mean, that, in whatever part of it I am, I judge it meet, right and my bounden duty, to declare unto all that are willing to hear, the glad tidings of salvation."

Since Aldersgate Renewal Ministries is on the Internet, requests come in from around the world for persons from ARM to come and minister in other countries. To date, ARM's Lord, Teach Us To Pray and/or Life in the Spirit seminars have been translated into the languages of the people and held in Russia, Estonia, Poland, Peru, Paraguay, Brazil, Tanzania, Liberia, Nepal, the Philippines, England, Slovakia, and India. In Tanzania, the Life in the Spirit seminar was held for United Methodists in two United Nations refugee camps— one for refugees from the Democratic Republic of the Congo, and one for refugees from Burundi. At the one held in the Burundian refugee camp, seven hundred people were at the seminar, the largest such seminar that ARM has ever held. The Lay Witness Mission has been held in South Africa, England, Canada, New Zealand, and Australia.

Chapter Four

TWENTIETH- AND TWENTY-FIRST-CENTURY MANIFESTATIONS OF THE SPIRIT AMONG METHODISTS

AZUZA STREET

CHARLES PARHAM IS known as the father of the modern-day Pentecostal movement. Parham became a Sunday school teacher in the local Methodist church, and by the age of fifteen he had held his own evangelistic meetings. At sixteen, he enrolled at Southwestern Kansas College, a Methodist school. He was licensed to preach by the Southwest Kansas Annual Conference in 1893. The following June, he became pastor of the Methodist church in Eudora, Kansas.[1] Parham definitely had Methodist roots, although he left the denomination.

There were some Methodist clergy in Charles Parham's student body of some forty people at Bethel Bible College in Topeka, Kansas, where he first prayed for Agnes Ozman to receive the Holy Spirit like in the Book of Acts on New Year's Day 1901.[2]

The man especially associated with the Asuza Street outpouring was William Seymour. He arrived in Indianapolis, Indiana, at the age of twenty-five and there joined the A. B. Simpson Chapel Methodist Episcopal Church. This branch of the northern Methodists had a strong evangelistic outreach to all classes, which appealed greatly to Seymour. It helped him formulate his belief that the church should be interracial.[3]

The 1905–1906 awakening in North America was part of a worldwide outpouring of the Holy Spirit beginning in Wales the previous year.[4] Because the North American revival actually originated with events in Wales, no American location can be identified as the center from which revival spread. As people received news of what was happening in Wales, the awakening soon became manifest in many locations.[5] There was revival among Methodists in Michigan and Schenectady, New York. There was revival at Asbury College in Wilmore, Kentucky, where E. Stanley Jones soon committed himself to missions. There was revival among Methodists in Indiana and in Houston, Texas.[6] A powerful revival came to the Lake Avenue Methodist Episcopal Church in Pasadena, California.[7]

Many people were praying for a move of God in Los Angeles before the fire of God fell on Azuza Street. A leading Methodist layman, commenting on Azuza Street, said, "The scenes transpiring here are what Los Angeles churches have been praying for for years. I have been a Methodist for twenty-five years. I was a leader of a prayer band for the First Methodist Church. We prayed that Pentecost might come to the city of Los Angeles. We wanted it to start in the First Methodist Church, but God did not start it there. I bless God that it did not start in any church in this city, but in a barn, so that we might all come and take part in it."[8]

In a similar statement, Mrs. Florence Crawford, who later founded the Apostolic Faith work in Portland, Oregon, said: "I was a Methodist and felt sure that the Spirit should be poured out upon us. Some of my friends were Baptist, Christian, and Missionary Alliance and others. We all said, 'Surely God will pour out His Spirit on our particular group.' But God had chosen the time, the place, and the people upon whom He would send His blessing and power."[9]

Ann Taves writes, "Many who were drawn to Azuza Street arrived by way of radical Holiness groups with Methodist roots.... William H. Durham, Holiness evangelist from Chicago...said that although he had attended 'many large holiness camp meetings and conventions,' he had never before felt 'the power and glory that I felt in Azuza Street Mission.'...One Tuesday afternoon, having become 'much disheartened, suddenly the power of God descended upon me, and I went down under it.' He lay for two hours 'under His mighty power,' but knew he had not yet received the baptism. The same thing happened again on Thursday night. On Friday evening, the power again came

over him and he 'jerked and quaked under it for about three hours.'
That night, Durham reported, 'He worked my whole body, one section at a time, first my arms, then my limbs, them my body, then my
head, then my face, then my chin, and finally at 1 a.m. Saturday, Mar.
2, after being under the power three hours, He finished the work on
my vocal organs and spoke through me in unknown tongues.'"[10]

When Durham returned to Chicago, a powerful Pentecostal revival
broke out at his North Avenue Mission. Historian Thomas William
Miller has written, "When Durham returned to Chicago, a Pentecostal
revival broke out which replicated, if it did not exceed, the supernatural events of the Azuza Street Mission. The North Avenue Mission
was so full of the power of God, according to eyewitnesses that 'a
thick haze...like blue smoke' filled its upper region. When this haze
was present...the people entering the building would fall down in the
aisles. Some never got to sit in the pews. Many came through to the
baptism or received divine healing.'"[11]

Ann Taves comments, "In the descriptions of Pentecostal worship
at Azuza Street...the biblical imagery and exegetical framework of
the Wesleyan camp meeting tradition was still prominently on display.
Other pan-Pentecostal motifs, more commonly noted in the literature,
were evident as well, but we miss the heart of worship at Azuza if
we lose sight of the primal Methodist desire to shout 'glory' in the
presence of God. To get at the Methodist contribution, it is important
to distinguish between the theological *content* of worship and theological reflections on its *form*. Although Methodist themes were less
prominent in the content of worship, the camp-meeting tradition provided a theology of worship."[12]

Quite a number of the big names in the Pentecostal and healing
revival at the end of the nineteenth and the first half of the twentieth century were Methodists or had Methodist connections at the
start. Examples are: Evans Roberts (1878–1951), Charles Parham (1873–
1929), William Seymore (1870–1922), John G. Lake (1870–1935), Smith
Wigglesworth (1859–1947), Aimee Semple McPherson (1890–1944),
Kathryn Kuhlman (1907–1976), Jack Coe (1918–1957), and A. A. Allen
(1911–1970). All of these folks left the Methodists.[13]

THE CHARISMATIC RENEWAL

The April 1960 issue of *Time* carried the story of an Episcopal priest in Van Nuys, California, who had announced to his congregation that he had been baptized in the Holy Spirit and had spoken in tongues. Many historians mark this as the beginning of the modern Charismatic Renewal. Like fire fanned by the wind, Pentecost spread quickly, penetrating most of the historic denominations, including the Methodists.

Also around 1960, Methodist pastor and evangelist Ben Johnson started the Lay Witness Mission movement. This powerful movement of God used laypeople sharing with other laypeople about their experiences with Jesus. Although these weekends focused on faith sharing, many of the team members and coordinators were Spirit-filled. And although the content of the weekend did not focus on the Holy Spirit, people became open to the Spirit, and the Holy Spirit often was manifested. Speaking in tongues and other manifestations of the Spirit were not uncommon at Lay Witness Missions. The Lay Witness Mission became part of the General Board of Discipleship of the UMC and at the height of the movement in 1973–74, 2,400 missions were scheduled, there were more than 100,000 team members on the rolls, with 1,200 Lay Witness Missions coordinators to use them.

In 1968, the Evangelical United Brethren Church (about 3 million members) and the Methodist Church (about 8 million members) merged to form the United Methodist Church. They adopted a new logo—the cross and the flame—for the new 11-million-member denomination. It fits our United Methodist history well—the message of the cross delivered with the power of the Spirit.

However, there was also a significant change in the process of affirming persons as preachers and elders that also took place at that time. Drs. Jim and Molly Scott point out in their book, *Restoring Methodism:*

> Up until the end of 1964, paragraph 302 in *Doctrines and Discipline of The United Methodist Church*, Part III, The Ministry, Chapter 1: "the Call to Preach," read: "In order that we may try those persons who profess to be moved by the Holy Spirit to preach, let the following questions be asked, namely: . . ." It went on to list the questions.

In addition to those questions, the person desiring to preach would be interviewed with a whole series of questions such as, "How has the Holy Spirit moved you? How did you know it was the Holy Spirit speaking to you? How will the Holy Spirit help you in your ministry? How do you understand the Person and Work of the Holy Spirit in Methodist ministry?" This questioning might have gone on for an hour or two.

In 1968, with the title now changed to *The Book of Discipline of the United Methodist Church*, the same paragraph in the same chapter was changed to read: "There are persons within the ministry of the baptized who are called of God and set apart by the Church for the specialized ministry of Word, Sacrament, and Order." The Holy Spirit was taken out of the equation.[14]

In the 2012 *Book of Discipline*, under the section on "The Meaning of Ordination and Conference Membership," paragraph 302 consists of 17 lines with no reference to the Holy Spirit. And paragraph 301 speaks of people who "respond to God's call by offering themselves in leadership as set-apart ministers." In a major sense, the nature of the call of the Holy Spirit has been weakened.

OFFICIAL RECOGNITION OF ALDERSGATE RENEWAL MINISTRIES

Many of the people renewed by the Lay Witness Mission in the '60s and '70s went to parachurch groups, like Full Gospel Businessmen's Fellowship or Women Aglow, or Camps Farthest Out or meetings held by Pentecostal churches and charismatic organizations to learn more about the Holy Spirit and manifestations. Many of these people were leaving Methodist churches for Pentecostal and independent charismatic churches. To stem this exodus, an official statement on the relationship between the United Methodist Church and the charismatic movement was needed. It would indicate to the church at large that Methodists with charismatic experiences were not an aberration and that they should be welcomed and nurtured. Such a position statement was requested at the 1972 General Conference, and the document

"Guidelines: The United Methodist Church and the Charismatic Movement" was approved by the 1976 General Conference. It was subsequently placed in the United Methodist *Book of Resolutions* at the 1996 and 2000 General Conferences.

In 1977, the Conference on Charismatic Renewal in the Christian Churches gathered at Kansas City and brought together an estimated fifty thousand persons from at least thirteen major Christian denominations (including an estimated eight hundred United Methodists) and up to forty smaller groups and networks. In the United Methodist sessions, the issue of the need for a national United Methodist charismatic fellowship group was discussed. It was opposed by the five leaders of the session, but they promised to pray about it for six weeks and report back by mail. During that time of prayer and discernment, they consulted with two bishops, who both encouraged them to form such a group. So, in 1978, the United Methodist Renewal Services Fellowship (UMRSF) was officially incorporated. The organization is now known as Aldersgate Renewal Ministries. The first National Aldersgate Conference was held at Louisville, Kentucky, in 1979. It assured people that you can be a born again, Spirit-filled Christian and remain a United Methodist. Over the years, the Aldersgate conference has become an annual reunion for Spirit-filled United Methodists from all over the country, and manifestations of the Spirit can be observed there.

The General Board of Discipleship accepted UMRSF as one of its affiliates, creating an official connection with the denomination.

In 1978, out of the Roman Catholic Cursillo movement, the Emmaus Walk program was instituted by the Upper Room section of the General Board of Discipleship. This spiritual reflection weekend, like the Lay Witness Mission, has also often opened Methodists to the working of the Holy Spirit. While not emphasized, manifestations of the Spirit are sometimes experienced during and after those weekends.

HISTORY OF THE LIFE IN THE SPIRIT SEMINAR

For a number of years, the Roman Catholic Church had a Life in the Spirit seminar, and many Catholics involved in the Catholic charismatic movement participated in that seminar.

Former ARM executive director Rev. Gary Moore developed his own version of the Life in the Spirit seminar at Bedford UMC in Texas, where he was on staff. It was specifically designed as a follow-up to Lay Witness Missions. Over time, it became part of the core curriculum for church membership classes in that church.

Gary was asked to bring this seminar to another United Methodist church in Campbellsville, Kentucky. He took a team of people with him, gave them each a section of the seminar to teach, and the first United Methodist Life in the Spirit seminar was taken "on the road."

In 1989, the Life in the Spirit seminar became a program offering of ARM. It was offered to churches across our country. It has been held in a women's prison and a men's prison.

Requests began coming in from around the world for this seminar. The Philippines was the first. Materials were translated into Chinese, and they went there. This seminar has been held in Russia, Paraguay, Poland, Peru, Nepal, Tanzania (including two refugee camps), Slovakia, Liberia, India, Brazil, Estonia, and England.

Aldersgate Renewal Ministries has come into a time of unprecedented favor among many leaders in the United Methodist Church. The 2004 General Conference referred the *Guidelines for the UMC and the Charismatic Movement* to the General Board of Discipleship for updating and reinsertion in 2008. ARM was called upon to do the major work on that revision. That revision was passed by the 2008 General Conference and appears in the 2008 and 2012 *Book of Resolutions.* (See Appendix 5.)

ARM has been resourcing local churches, districts, annual conferences, and international venues with teaching, programs, and events on spiritual renewal and the Holy Spirit. It continues to provide teaching to the church that interprets manifestations of the Spirit from a Wesleyan perspective.

OTHER LOCAL CHURCH RENEWAL
EVENTS PROVIDED BY ARM

Margie Burger, director of prayer ministries at ARM, developed two local church renewal events on prayer. Lord, Teach Us to Pray is a team-led weekend focusing on the individual's prayer life. It encourages participants to become people of prayer. It challenges people to mature in their prayer life and to walk in intimacy with God. (See www.lordteachustoprayseminar.com.)

Pathways to a Praying Church is a team-led weekend seminar designed to encourage participants to pray together corporately. It equips churches to become houses of prayer, and it equips people with the tools for a consistent, powerful prayer life. (See www.pathwaystoaprayingchurch.com.)

Worship in Spirit and Truth was designed by Jonathan Dow, executive director of ARM, as a team-led weekend to give participants a biblical understanding of worship. Incorporating Scripture from both the Old and New Testaments, teachings given by team members examine both corporate worship experiences and the lives of individual worshipers. (See www.worshipinspiritandtruthseminar.com.)

For over fifty years, the Lay Witness Mission has been a tool used by God to bring people to new and renewed commitments to Jesus Christ in Methodist churches and other denominations in the United States and in other countries around the world. In 2003, the General Board of Discipleship discontinued the Lay Witness program, and in 2004 they gave it and its follow-up event, Venture in Discipleship, to ARM to update and continue. Now ARM coordinates Lay Witness Mission and Venture in Discipleship events all over the country. (See www.laywitnessmission.com and www.ventureindiscipleship.com.)

The newest local church renewal event offered by ARM is the Supernatural Ministry seminar. Flowing out of ARM's Methodist School for Supernatural Ministry, this event allows a local church to custom-design a weekend on supernatural ministry that will develop new ministries or strengthen existing ones. In addition to teaching on subjects chosen by the church, participants get an opportunity to put into practice what they have learned. (See www.supernaturalministryseminar.com.)

METHODIST SCHOOL FOR SUPERNATURAL MINISTRY

In 1994, Vineyard pastor Randy Clark came and spoke at the Toronto Airport Christian Fellowship (now Catch the Fire Toronto), and revival broke out. Over a ten-year period, over 5 million people came through the doors of the church and over sixty thousand unbelievers found salvation in Jesus Christ.[15] United Methodists have been among the 5 million who have come through the doors of that church and who have been touched by that ministry.

Because United Methodists were experiencing supernatural ministry at Toronto, or Brownsville in Pensacola, or International House of Prayer in Kansas City, or with Global Awakening, or with Bethel Church in Redding, California, or any of a number of other outpourings and ministries, it seemed right to the leadership of ARM to start a Methodist School of Supernatural Ministry in October 2010. ARM wanted United Methodists to know that there were other United Methodists who believed that God still moves supernaturally today. One doesn't have to leave the United Methodist Church to experience supernatural ministry.

The first four sessions of the four-day-long schools have addressed such topics as the supernatural history of Methodism, intimacy with God, being baptized in the Holy Spirit, moving in the anointing, hearing God, prophecy, dreams and visions, inner healing, physical healing, deliverance, raising the dead, being transported in the Spirit, angelic encounters, and other supernatural topics. (For more information go to www.supernaturalmethodist.com. New sessions are already in the planning stages.)

Two hundred different people from twenty-three different states came to the Aldersgate Renewal Center in Goodlettsville, Tennessee, for these sessions. Others watched on the webstream. The sessions were videotaped and put on DVDs. Individuals and churches have purchased those DVDs to be used in homes and Bible studies, and testimonies have come in about how God has "shown up" in those settings while people were viewing the DVDs. The DVDs have been sent to eight different countries around the world, including one that is a hot bed for al Qaeda.

UNITED THEOLOGICAL SEMINARY

United Theological Seminary in Dayton, Ohio, is one of the United Methodist Church's thirteen official seminaries. God is doing a supernatural work in transforming United from a dying liberal seminary to a vibrant Spirit-filled seminary focused on the renewal of the church. Dr. Peter Bellini, professor of Missiology at United, contacted ARM about wanting to develop a partnership with ARM. He asked if United could offer the Methodist School for Supernatural Ministry DVDs as a non-degree online course. This was agreed to, and the first session began in August 2012.

Peter went on to ask if ARM would partner with United in offering a three-year, fully accredited doctor of ministry course in supernatural ministry. This was also agreed to, and that course began in January 2013. No other accredited seminary in the United States is offering such a degree.

WHAT ABOUT IN UNITED METHODIST CHURCHES TODAY?

Contemporary church-growth guru Tom Bandy, writing in the September/October 2007 issue of *Circuit Rider*, said that there are big shifts changing church life and mission for years to come, and among those shifts, he mentions, "There will be more stories of miracles, supernatural connections, and mystical expressions of the real presence of Jesus the Christ."[16]

Those stories are now coming from American United Methodist churches.

At Washington Crossing UMC in Washington Crossing, Pennsylvania, they have had 240 people go through an Experiencing the Presence of God class. At the end of one of the classes for high school students, the leader had gold dust on his hand and pants. The students heard clearly from God and some had visions. The church's healing rooms and worship services have yielded testimonies of physical healings weekly.

A team from the outpouring at Lakeland, Florida, came to First UMC, Salem, Massachusetts, in the city that had been the center for the Salem witch trials and has become a center for satanic activity. Someone at the Lakeland meeting received a prophecy from the Lord that said God was going to take back Salem. In this United Methodist church in Salem, they had praise and worship and Holy Communion. They reaffirmed the original Salem Covenant that was Christian through and through and told Satan and his demons that he was through in that town. There were healings. One of our ARM board members at that time was in that meeting and saw a glory cloud in that church. It was translucent, multi-colored, glowing, and moving within itself like breathing.

Ogden UMC in Princeton, Kentucky, and the Madisonville District of the UMC created the Prayer Center, a ministry connected with the church. Director Kathy Hershman there says, "We have had thousands of visitors—from all over the US and many, many foreign countries. Our visitors are from all denominations—even Messianic Jews."

Kathy reports, "It is a prayer place like you've probably not seen. Every room has a theme. You can see the rooms on our web site." (See www.theprayercenter.us.) "We found that all you need to do is take some old paint, add a little anointing oil, sanctify it as holy—and God does the rest. It is in an old building in bad shape. But God hangs out there.

"Some of the things that have happened include:

- A cloud in the Ark of the Covenant Room 5 or 6 times. The first time was right before we opened and the district pastors were doing a tour.

- Smells are not uncommon. The most common is the smell of baking bread filling the place.

- We have had to disconnect the smoke alarms because when the presence of God comes in strongly the alarms go off.

- Quite often we walk through the place and pray and anoint it with oil. Once for about 2–3 weeks every place that we had anointed—the oil began to re-appear. Not only did it re-appear, but it reproduced. So there was oil running everywhere.

- We have a "wailing wall" made out of styrofoam. Whenever kids and teens (why them?) put their hands on it the "rocks" get hot. Makes no sense with styrofoam.

- One day when I was praying for a woman, her hands filled with oil.

- Sometimes I find my face and hands covered with gold dust.

- People have seen manifested angels—including myself once.

- Sometimes people fall out when they get to the top of the steps. The funniest time was when the state and county prayer coordinators for the National Day of Prayer came. Everyone who walked into the Pool of Bethesda room fell out and got holy laughter. Had to explain later to the Baptists what had happened to them.

- We also do healing prayer ministry. We have seen a lot of great miracles happen. The question that we always hear is— *And you're Methodists???*"

United Methodists Rush and Barbie Hunt started Healing Rooms of Hopkins County in 2009 at the Main Street Prayer Center in Madisonville, Kentucky. (See www.mainstreetprayer.org.) There they have experienced all kinds of miraculous healings. Within a year of their opening, more than one hundred people from twelve different churches had been trained and released to pray for the sick and hurting. Three years later, they had had more than two thousand prayer sessions, where hundreds were healed, set free, and encouraged. They trained hundreds of people all over Kentucky and beyond and helped to open ten other healing rooms in Kentucky, with more in the making.

The Hunts love to train children to be part of healing prayer teams. Barbie has even written a book to be used in training children to do this. She reports on the activities of one of their children's prayer teams:

A lady who had received prayer before came in with a migraine so bad she had been to the doctor, had four pills in two days, and a shot, but nothing had helped. This particular time we had an adult in the hall with the door open because the children wanted to pray without adults in the room. She was in such pain; it was very evident on her face when she came in. Ages 4, 5, 8 & 10 wanted to be on the same team. She looked real bad. The 8-year-old saw the chart and saw the word headache and just said, "Oh, headache, no problem." Both of the adults kept their mouths shut. We did not say what we were thinking. We wanted to explain to the children how serious a migraine is but we did not, because they had more faith than we did. They went in and prayed for about 10 minutes, then the 5-year-old came to the intercession room to get the shofar. It is big, four feet long, and soon we heard loud sounds coming from the room. All four can blow it well! The lady followed the kids, all running back into the intercession room happy. She was laughing as she said when they blew the shofar in her ear, the migraine just blew out! She left pain free and laughing.

Barbie goes on to say:

One of our team members went to church the next Sunday and told the story of the shofar during the sharing time at this small congregation, and how we call people and they are healed over the phone. For the very first time during Sunday morning church they called a member who was too sick to attend. The whole church prayed over the phone. One of our Healing Rooms kids goes to that church so she got the shofar and blew it over the phone. The lady felt waves of healing over her body. She had the most terrible case of shingles you can imagine. The next Sunday she was in church, and within two weeks she was totally healed, without doing anything but walk out the miracle of that Sunday. She says it was a breakthrough when the church called and she heard that shofar over the phone.[17]

Numbers of UMCs in western Kentucky are experiencing increased healings and other supernatural phenomena in their churches. Shane Browning is a western Kentucky United Methodist pastor currently in a "leave" situation because God has called him to work with the city of Madisonville on city reform. He prayed on a Sunday for a twelve-year-old who was in a wheelchair since birth. The boy stood and walked—not just walked, but *really* walked. The boy woke up Monday morning as if he had never been in a wheelchair. He spent the whole day swimming. On Wednesday, Shane prayed for a ten-year-old girl who had been in an automobile accident three years ago. She had been totally blinded. Her sight was restored.

Rev. Rob Fearneyhough, who retired from Gracewood UMC outside Augusta, Georgia, reports:

> I have seen and heard about rain in sanctuaries throughout the years. Ours was more of a mist that lasted for several minutes. Others have given testimony of rain, demonstrating what was happening in the spiritual was corresponding to the natural, as the Lord rained down His Spirit upon those gathered. The Gracewood congregation has experienced feathers, gold teeth, and gold dust as well.
>
> Several times the Gracewood congregation has had glory clouds come into the sanctuary with the heaviness of His Presence. There was a similar glory cloud over Arrowhead Stadium at the 1977 Charismatic Conference in Kansas City. It was about the same size as the perimeter of the stadium and hovered over the stadium as we were leaving the first meeting of the Conference. The prophetic word at Kansas City was "Repent, for my body is broken." Most went to their knees and tears and weeping were heard throughout the stadium.

In his retirement, Rev. Fearneyhough has begun a school of supernatural ministry in Augusta. (See www.muchmoreministries.com.)

Pastor Keith Michaels of First United Methodist in Carlyle, Illinois, reports that at their church they have a "Miracle Wall" where they record God's miraculous answers to prayer.

In the Holston Annual Conference, Rev. Ken Sprinkle reports on some of the supernatural work of the Holy Spirit in his churches:

> We have seen God move since our first Sunday. I had a "Word of Knowledge" through discomfort in my right leg just behind the knee at the end of the service in my Falls Mills Church. A woman responded (she told her daughter standing next to her "That's my knee!"), and that afternoon posted her healing on Facebook! She gave testimony the next week.
>
> The past two Sundays at the Virginia Avenue Church two people (one each Sunday) have been healed of migraine headaches that they were experiencing at that moment. The first

was in response to a Word of Knowledge, the second when a woman came forward for prayer and anointing. The headaches were gone by the end of the services. Both have testified now. Other reports of answers to prayer and healing from Prayer Cloths are coming in weekly. This is new to the people in these churches, but a Sunday does not go by without someone being anointed with oil or receiving a Prayer Cloth. A twelve-year old got a prayer cloth for her grandfather, who the doctors thought had lung cancer. Reports back from biopsies say that they can't find cancer—what they saw on the scans has "turned out" to be scar tissue. Another man had back surgery a couple of weeks ago, and when he got back to his room became very agitated, and was searching all through his hospital gown. When asked what was wrong he replied, "I can't find my Prayer Cloth! It was in the pocket of my gown and it's not there now." (Of course, gowns had been changed during surgery.) He was quieted only by the family telling him that the surgery was over and the Prayer Cloth did its work. He's home and walking around now, promised by the doctor that he will be able to play golf again in the spring (he's in his 70s).

A woman with MS has noticed improvement in the past 2 month as she has been anointed several times (I told her to come forward every time she feels the need for a touch from God). Father God is also healing inside stuff, which may also contribute to the physical healing! She testified last night (at a Nominations Committee meeting) to healing improvement in her body. (We had revival at that meeting—three testimonies in all!) For every UM Pastor, what a word of hope and encouragement—that the Spirit can move in a Nominations Committee!

When photos were taken of the youth at the Aldersgate Renewal Ministries national Aldersgate conference in 2008 and 2009, many showed tongues of fire over the youth when they were praying or worshipping. Several participants in Aldersgate 2008, 2009, and 2010 conferences reported gold dust showing up on them.

We have received a number of testimonies from people who attended sessions of the ARM Methodist School for Supernatural Ministry about God working in supernatural ways in their churches when they got home. We have also received similar testimonies from people who have purchased the DVDs of those sessions and used them in their homes or in small groups with their churches. And we have received testimonies of God ministering to people over the webstream or on cell phones as the school was going on.

Then there is my own United Methodist granddaughter Leila. In her first two years, her parents would often find gold dust on her head when she woke up in the morning. When she was three, she walked up to a lady in church sitting by herself and looking rather depressed. She did not know the lady, but she said to her, "I know your mommy left you, but your Daddy loves you." And then Leila just walked off and continued to do her three-year-old thing. The lady burst into tears. She had been abandoned by her mother and was feeling very alone and down. Leila had spoken a prophetic word into her life at three!

She is now eight. She was walking by the glass doors of their church sanctuary with her daddy one day and said, "Oh, look, Daddy. There are angels dancing in the sanctuary!" He could not see them, but he turned to her and said, "Tell me everything you know about angels!"

They were ministering in the Chicago area, and during the time of ministry after the worship and message, Leila went up to this one lady who was seeking prayer and asked her "Can I pray for you?" And the lady thought, "Isn't that sweet! This little girl wants to pray for me." So she said, "Sure, honey, you can pray for me." So Leila told her, "Well, you see that lady standing right there? There's a big angel standing right behind her and she is going to fall right here so we need to move over a bit." Just then, the lady did fall over into that spot. And the lady turned to Leila and said, "*Please* pray for me!"

Leila has been seeing Jesus appearing next to people during ministry time. So her parents started a new game with Leila that they call "Where's Jesus?" They have told her that when she sees Jesus appear next to someone, she should go over to that person and do what Jesus is doing. So sometimes she will see Jesus kneel next to the person—and she will do that. Sometimes she will see Jesus lay hands on the person—and she will do that. Sometimes she will see Jesus lay prostrate on the ground next to the person—and she will do that. And most of the time when she does, this the person will fall over under the power of God.

One day her mother was not feeling well and was not going to be able to minister with her husband at a service that night. So Leila said to her, "Don't worry, Mommy. You stay home, and I will go with Daddy and bring the anointing!"

Leila's older brothers, Christian (twelve) and Forrest (eleven) also pray for the sick, deliver words of knowledge, prophesy, and help their parents lead worship.

HEALING AMONG UNITED METHODISTS TODAY

The United Methodist hymnal has a section of hymns and prayers for healing. The *2008 UM Book of Worship* approved by the General Conference has healing services in it. The Upper Room supplemental worship book also has healing services in it. Abington Press published a whole book of healing services by James Wagner. When he was on staff of the General Board of Discipleship, Wagner wrote a book called *Blessed to Be a Blessing*[18] on how to get a healing ministry started in your local church. He also developed a weekend event called Adventure in Healing and Wholeness, where trained instructors would go to local churches to teach on healing ministry. That has now been published as a "do it yourself" manual.[19]

There are United Methodist healing evangelists and United Methodists regularly involved in healing, like those listed below:

- Gary & Marcia Ball (www.bridgebuildersforhim.com)
- Rick Bonfim (www.latterain.com)
- Shane Browning (www.lifecoach-consultants.com)
- Bobby Cabot (Kingdom Life Healing Ministries, 28 Caberfae Hwy, Manistee, MI 49660; klhmbobby@yahoo.com)
- Larry & Audrey Eddings (www.wosm-nw.org)
- Taylor and Jenny Gallman (www.discovergodscall.org)
- Tommy Hays (www.messiah-ministries.org)

- David Oliver (www.livingh2oministries.com)

- Richard Rhodes (www.fireinthemountains.com)

Margie Burger's Pathways to a Praying Church weekend ARM local church renewal event has "Teaching a Church to Pray for Healing" as one of its components.

There are United Methodist churches that have regular healing services or healing ministries. Just a few are listed below:

- Bluefield, VA (www.virginiaavenueumc.com)

- East Stone Gap, VA (www.esgumc.com)

- Kent Island, MD (www.kiumc.org; contact Chris Johnston)

- Main Street Prayer Center, KY (www.mainstreetprayer.org)

- Midway Locust Grove, Columbia, MO (www.midwaylocust-grove.com)

- Princeton Prayer Center, KY (www.theprayercenter.us)

- Sugar Hill, GA (www.sugarhillumc.org)

- Washington Crossing, PA (www.crossingumc.org)

- Windsor Village, TX (www.kingdombuilders.com)

If you Google "United Methodist Healing Ministry," the search results will give you many UMCs that list healing ministries on their websites.

In the 2012 *Book of Resolutions* of the UMC, Resolution 3202 Health and Wholeness, under "The Call to United Methodists," it states: "We call upon our members to: continue the redemptive ministry of Christ, including teaching, preaching, and healing. Christ's healing was not peripheral but central in his ministry. As the church, therefore, we understand ourselves to be called by the Lord to the holistic ministry of healing: spiritual, mental, emotional, and physical."

At my church, we have anointing with oil and prayer for healing as a part of every monthly Communion service. When I first came to this church eight years ago, they had no background in anointing with oil or laying on of hands for healing. I didn't know any way to ease into this, so on a Communion Sunday, early in my first year there, I gave some teaching on anointing with oil and laying on of hands and healing and just announced that as we went into the Communion service, if anyone had a need for healing themselves or a concern for another person needing healing, we wanted to pray for them. So as they knelt for Communion, after they received the bread and cup, if they had a need for healing prayer, they were invited to hold out their hand in a receiving mode and I would come and anoint them with oil and pray for that need.

Being the great man of faith that I am, I told my wife, Peg, ahead of time that she *would* have a need for healing, to ask for prayer for that morning so people would be assured of seeing this happen. To my surprise, at least half of the people coming for Communion also asked for anointing for healing for themselves or someone else. And since that time, people ask for anointing at every Communion service. I have never had one Communion service since the start where no one asked for anointing.

At first I did all the anointing and praying for healing. Now my lay leader does one side and I do the other. And I have another lady that is moving toward being ready to do this as well.

For most of my ministry, I gave a Communion table "dismissal" for each group as they finished receiving Communion at the Communion rail that consisted of a scripture sentence or two and a blessing. Now I prophesy over each group whatever words God gives me to speak.

Today, some 70 million people around the world call themselves Methodists and trace their history back to the supernatural ministry of John Wesley. Many of the Methodists outside Europe and the United States still believe in and experience supernatural ministry on a regular basis.

Chapter Five

WHY ARE SIGNS AND WONDERS IMPORTANT?

FRANCIS MacNUTT HAS written, "To Jesus, healing and deliverance were not merely 'signs and wonders'; together with preaching, they were the central focus of His Kingdom message.... 'The Kingdom of God is at hand; the kingdom of evil is being destroyed' forms the basic teaching of Christianity. As [1 John 3:8] tells us, 'the reason the Son of God appeared was to destroy the devil's work.'"[1]

Jesus said that the kingdom of God is at hand and the kingdom of God is in your midst. What do we really think happens when the kingdom of God is in our midst? Although it is true that we will not experience the fullness of that kingdom until after we die, when God will wipe away every tear and there will be no more crying or pain, Jesus also preached that the kingdom is present with us now. He told us to pray, "Thy kingdom come, Thy will be done on earth as it is in heaven." So along with proclaiming the kingdom of God is at hand, we need to proclaim that the kingdom of Satan is being destroyed. That is the other side of the good news.

In the first chapter of Mark, we read how Jesus met a man with an unclean spirit that cried out, "What do you want with us, Jesus of Nazareth? Have you come to destroy us?" And although Jesus chose not to enter into conversation with a demon, his clear answer to the question would be, "You got that right! I *have* come to destroy you and all the devil's works!" What is interesting here is the response of the people. Mark 1:27 says that the people were amazed and said, "A new teaching, and with authority." There is no record of Jesus giving a lecture on casting out demons here, yet the people referred to a new teaching. They recognized that this was not just a spectacular event, not just signs and wonders; there was a new teaching here. The kingdom of Satan was being destroyed. And this teaching was being taught through actions.

Signs and wonders are often portrayed as being done as enticements for people to believe or to prove who Jesus was. And there is biblical support for that. Peter addressed his hearers at Pentecost, saying, "Jesus of Nazareth was a man accredited by God to you by miracles, wonders and signs, which God did among you through Him, as you yourselves know" (Acts 2:22). And John wrote in his Gospel, "A great crowd of people followed Him because they saw the miraculous signs He had performed on the sick" (John 6:2), and in verse 14, "After the people saw the miraculous sign that Jesus did, they began to say, 'Surely this is the Prophet who is to come into the world.'" But it is important to see that the miracles were part of the message itself. They expressed the mission of Jesus as our Savior—one who would save us from all the works of the devil—sin, sickness, demonic oppression, being spiritually lost, and more.

Miracles express the very nature of Jesus and of God. We follow a supernatural God—a God who does not hesitate to intervene in our world in ways that appear to us as supernatural. Wasn't that Elijah's challenge to the prophets of Baal? He set up the terms of the test and then waited to see which God would intervene supernaturally. The real God would be the supernatural God.

Paul said that preaching words was not enough. Preaching was to be linked to demonstrations of the power of God. He wrote to the Corinthians, "My message and my preaching were not with wise and persuasive words, but with a demonstration of the Spirit's power, so that your faith might not rest on men's wisdom, but on God's power" (1 Cor. 2:4). And again, "For the kingdom of God is not a matter of talk but of power" (1 Cor. 4:20). He wrote to the Thessalonians, "Our gospel came to you not simply with words, but also with power, with the Holy Spirit and with deep conviction" (1 Thess. 1:5).

In Acts 14, in Lystra, a town in Galatia, Paul heals a man who was crippled from birth, and Luke says that the reaction of the people was that they said the gods had come down in human form. They called Barnabas *Zeus,* and Paul they called *Hermes.* Pagan priests wanted to bring sacrifices to them. In a letter to those Galatians, Paul says that they welcomed him as an angel of God, as if he were Christ Jesus himself (Gal. 4:14). Perhaps he was referring to this incident in the Book of Acts. In any case, to be welcomed like an angel or like Jesus Himself implies that signs and wonders occurred. But then in verse 19, Paul says "It is like I am in the pains of childbirth until Christ is formed in you."

What does it mean for Christ to be formed in you? When that forming process is done, what would the end result look like?

- Is Christ fully formed in you when you become a kind and gentle person of good moral character? Was Jesus just a good guy?

- Is Christ fully formed in you when you teach and preach the truth of God? Was Jesus just a good moral teacher and preacher?

- Is Christ fully formed in you when you do acts of mercy for the poor, the imprisoned, the widows, and the orphans? Was Jesus just a doer of good deeds?

Jesus *was* these things, but He was more. He was also one who demonstrated both the advancement of the kingdom of God and the destruction of the kingdom of the devil in signs and wonders. And I would suggest that Christ is not fully formed in us until people see the *whole* Jesus in us.

Paul also calls us ambassadors for Christ (2 Cor. 5:20). An ambassador is a person who is a citizen of one kingdom living in another kingdom and who lives in that foreign kingdom representing the king of their homeland. Our king is Jesus. Our homeland is heaven. We represent Jesus to the world. We *re-present* Jesus. What Jesus do we re-present? As Bill Johnson says, "God cannot be properly or even accurately represented without power. Miracles are absolutely necessary for people to see Him clearly. They are an expression of our King's nature and they are an expression of His kingdom."[2]

In Romans 15:18-19, Paul says, "I will not venture to speak of anything except what Christ has accomplished through me in leading the Gentiles to obey God by what I have said *and done—by the power of signs and miracles, through the power of the Spirit.* So from Jerusalem all the way around to Illyricum, I have *fully proclaimed* the gospel of Christ" (emphasis added). Paul's effectiveness with the Gentiles was due not just to his words, but also to God's supernatural acts through him. I think we have not *fully proclaimed* the gospel without also demonstrating the power of signs and miracles, through the power of the Spirit.

In Ephesians 4:13, Paul looks forward to people becoming "mature, attaining to *the whole measure of the fullness of Christ*" (emphasis added). The whole measure of the fullness of Christ could not possibly leave out the signs, wonders, and miracles that Jesus did in His ministry! The "mature" disciple would be expected to be evidencing this ministry like Jesus did.

In 1 John 2:3, John writes, "We know that we have come to know Him *if we obey his commands*" (emphasis added). Did Jesus not command His disciples in Matthew 10:7-8, "As you go, preach this message: 'The kingdom of heaven is near.' Heal the sick, raise the dead, cleanse those who have leprosy, drive out demons." How well do we know Jesus if we are not following His command there?

And John continues, "Whoever claims to live in him *must walk as Jesus did*" (1 John 2:6, emphasis added). The New Living Translation says, "Those who say they live in God *should live their lives as Christ did*" (emphasis added). So, how did Jesus walk? How did Jesus live His life? Did He just demonstrate the fruit of the Spirit that Paul mentions in Galatians 5? Did He just love children, eat with tax collectors and sinners, and forgive people of their sins? Of course He did all that, but He did so much more. He lived His life, He walked, and He demonstrated that the kingdom of God had invaded earth through signs, wonders, and miracles. As He walked, blind people received their sight, crippled people walked, demons screamed and fled, storms were stilled. Nicodemus was led to say, "Rabbi, we know you are a teacher who has come from God. For no one could perform the miraculous signs you are doing if God were not with him" (John 3:2). Are we walking as Jesus did? Are we living our lives as Christ did?

Our English word *gospel* comes from the Old and Middle English *God spell* or *Good spell*. Although we think of that word as referring one of the first four books of the New Testament or a verbal message that Jesus died for our sins that we might receive eternal life, it actually came from what happened when Patrick of Ireland and other Spirit-filled believers encountered the Druids in England in the Middle Ages. The Druids practiced supernatural "ministry"—*bad spells.* Saint Patrick and his cohorts countered the Druids and their work with supernatural ministry from God—signs, wonders, and miracles, a *"God spell"* or *"Good spell."* It is a shame that our word *gospel* became just a verbal or written message and lost its original meaning of a message given through supernatural actions. When Patrick would preach the "God spell" or the "Good spell," it was words and supernatural actions linked together. People responded to their words because they were backed up with supernatural actions. Christ was formed in him. He re-presented Jesus.

Our English word *gospel* is used to translate the Greek *evangel,* which means *good news.* And it *is* good news, indeed. Not just a book (Matthew, Mark, Luke, or John), not just a message, but a message linked to actions demonstrating that the kingdom of God is advancing and the kingdom of the devil is being destroyed.

IS IT RIGHT TO SEEK SIGNS, WONDERS AND MIRACLES?

So, is it proper to ask for signs and wonders? Is it right to seek signs and wonders and miracles and manifestations of the power of God? I think the answer is: It depends. It depends on the heart attitude of the one asking. When God called Moses to bring His people out of Egypt and lead them through the wilderness, Moses told God, "I need a sign or they won't believe me." So God gave him a sign. He told Moses to take Aaron's rod and throw it down on the ground and it would turn into a snake and then pick it up again and it will turn back into the wooden rod (Num. 17:1–8). Moses' heart attitude was that he wanted to obey God.

Gideon asked God for a sign—a wet sheepskin and dry ground, and a dry sheepskin and wet ground (Judg. 6:36–40). And God granted that. Gideon's heart attitude was that he wanted to obey God.

The prophet Habakkuk cried out to God, "We have heard of your great deeds of the past. Do them again God. Do them in our time. In our time make them known" (Hab. 3:2). He was asking God to do the signs and wonders and miracles of power and deliverance that He did in the past again in Habakkuk's time because Habakkuk longed to see the reign of God in his day. But again, his desire for signs and wonders and miracles was coming from a perspective of faith.

God Himself spoke to believing but fearful king Ahaz, saying, "Ask the Lord your God for a sign, whether in the deepest depths or in the highest heights" (Isa. 7:11).

And in Acts 4:30, the disciples actually prayed for signs and wonders and miracles. They prayed, "Stretch out your hand to heal and perform miraculous signs and wonders through the name of your holy servant Jesus." And it says that after they prayed that prayer, the place where they were was shaken and they were all filled with the Holy Spirit and spoke the Word of God boldly. It seems that God accepted their prayer! They were praying from a heart focused on God and wanting to see His kingdom advance and the kingdom of Satan destroyed.

Our own John Wesley prayed for signs. If after he preached his messages he saw no manifestation of the power of God moving on the people, contemporary John Cennick noted that Wesley would cry out, "O Lord, where are your tokens and signs!"[3]

Looking back over his ministry and the displays of supernatural manifestations that he observed, Wesley wrote, "The danger *was* to regard *extraordinary* circumstances too much, such as outcries, convulsions, visions, trances, as if these were *essential* to the inward work, so that it *could not* go on without them. Perhaps (now) the danger *is* to regard them too little, to condemn them altogether, to imagine they had nothing of God in them and were an hindrance to the work."[4]

Wesley summarized his views in response to those who regarded the manifestations too little by writing: "The truth is (1) God suddenly and strongly convinced many that they were lost sinners, the *natural* consequences whereof were sudden outcries, and strong bodily convulsions. (2) To strengthen and encourage them that believed, and to make his work more apparent, He favoured several of them with divine dreams, others with trances and visions. (3) In some of these instances, after a time, nature mixed with grace. (4) Satan likewise mimicked *this work of God* in order to discredit the *whole work*."[5]

Even where people pretended to be moved by the Spirit or they imitated the movement of the Spirit in others, Wesley said, "Even this should not make us either deny nor undervalue the real work of the Spirit. The shadow is no disparagement of the substance, nor the counterfeit of the real diamond."[6]

So, what about the places where Jesus speaks against seeking signs and wonders? Places like Matthew 12:39, where Jesus says, "A wicked and adulterous generation seeks a sign." There are at least six such places in the gospels (see also Matt. 16:4; Mark 8:12; Luke 11:16, 29; John 2:18; 6:30, 64–66). But note that in each of these cases, Jesus was talking to or about unbelieving scribes and Pharisees or Herod. They were not asking for signs from a perspective of faith. They did not seek to see the kingdom of God advancing and manifesting itself in our world. They just wanted to see something to "wow" them.

These were the same folks who, when they saw the formerly dead Lazarus walking around, they got together to find a way to put him back in the grave quietly. And when they saw the lame man was healed by Peter and John at the entrance to the temple, Acts 4 says they conferred together and said, "Everybody living in Jerusalem knows they have done an outstanding miracle, and we cannot deny it. But to stop this thing from spreading any further among the people, we must warn these men to speak no longer to anyone in this name." They actually witnessed signs, wonders, and miracles but were unchanged. It was these people whom Jesus told not to seek signs, because they were seeking them apart from a relationship with God.

Jesus told us, "When you pray, pray like this: 'Thy kingdom come, thy will be done on earth as it is in heaven'" (Matt. 6:10). He was saying, "Pray for a manifestation of the conditions as they exist in heaven here *on* earth. Pray for the advancement of the kingdom of God, where the King reigns and the King's will is done, here on earth, as it is in heaven." Here on earth, that will often look like a sign or wonder or miracle. But not in heaven. People are not miraculously healed from illness in heaven because there is no sickness there. Demons are not cast out of people in heaven because there are no demons there. People are not raised from the dead there because they have already beaten death. Lepers are not cleansed with their body parts restored in heaven because there is no leprosy in heaven.

Here's the clincher! Remember what Jesus said in John 14:12? "I tell you the truth, anyone who has faith in me will do what I have been doing. He will do even greater things than these, because I am going to the Father."

I have heard people say, "We are to seek Jesus, not signs." OK. That's fine. It is absolutely true that we must not lose our focus on Jesus. Intimacy with Jesus is essential. But we are still stuck with what Jesus says about doing what He had been doing, which clearly included signs, wonders, and miracles. If we are seeking intimacy with Jesus and our lives still don't line up with what Jesus said they should look like, I am prompted to ask a Dr. Phil question: *So, how is that working for you?*

Why Is the History of the Supernatural Moves of God Important?

Why is God's history of working with His people important? History is "His Story." It is the story of what God has done in and through and for human beings.

A story has a plot, characters, theme—a beginning, middle, and end. A story has an author. These are also true of His Story. A testimony is a record of what God has done in the past. It is a written or spoken record that is part of His Story. We sometimes use the word *testimony* to mean how we came to put our faith in Christ or how we experienced a miracle, but God is the main character in a testimony. It is a story of what God has done.

Revelation 19:10 says, "The testimony of Jesus is the spirit of prophecy." The testimony of what Jesus has done in the past prophesies what God wants to do in the present and future. Such testimony reveals God's nature and intent—what He is like and what He wants to do.

When we read of God's supernatural acts in the Scriptures, they tell us that we serve a God whose very nature is supernatural, a God who is not limited by conditions on earth. We serve a God who does signs and wonders and miracles. And we read that Jesus Christ is the same yesterday, today, and forever (Heb. 13:8), so we can expect that same God to act in the same way today.

If I have cancer and I hear someone testify of how Jesus healed them of cancer, that testimony of Jesus prophesies hope into my life—that if Jesus did that for them, He can do it for me. What He has done in the past, He is willing to do today.

Beyond that, remembering the supernatural acts of God in the Scriptures, in church history, in our denomination's history, and in our own past sustains our ability to move in the miraculous today.

Bill Johnson writes, "Our capacity to remember what God has said and done in our lives and throughout history—the testimony—is one of the primary things that determines our success or failure in sustaining a kingdom lifestyle of power for miracles."[7]

Deuteronomy 6:17 states, "You shall diligently keep the commandments of the Lord your God, His testimonies, and his statutes, which he has commanded you" (NKJV). Keeping God's commandments and statutes seems rather clear, but how do we keep His testimonies? The work used there for *keep*, according to Strong's concordance, means "to guard in the sense of keeping your eye on someone or something." You are watching something or focusing on something. You don't want to lose it or let it get away.

So, God was telling the people to keep their eyes focused and their minds centered on the testimonies of His supernatural acts on their behalf in the past. By focusing on God's acts, we can train ourselves to see reality from God's perspective.

All through the Psalms, we read David speaking of the works of God, and in Psalm 111:2, he says, "The works of the Lord are great, studied by all who have pleasure in them." In Psalm 66:5-6, he shows how he studied and meditated on the works of God: "Come and see the works of God; He is awesome in his doing toward the sons of men. He turned the sea into dry land; they went through the river on foot. There we will rejoice in him."

Although these events David refers to occurred hundreds of years before his time, David finds that in studying them, he finds his faith strengthened that this same God will act on his behalf. In fact, the word translated *studied* in Psalm 111:2 can also mean "to seek after, to pursue." So David is saying that he would "seek after" and "pursue" the works of God until he personally experienced them—until he knew them not just from their being recorded in history but in his own experience.

Jesus led His disciples again and again into experiences with the miraculous. Being swept up in a powerful storm on the Sea of Galilee. Dealing with over five thousand hungry people with just a few loaves and fishes to feed them. Encountering the blind, the deaf, the lame, the demonized, and the lepers. Facing the death of Jesus' friend, Lazarus. Humanly impossible situations were opportunities for miracles. He wanted them to learn the ways of the kingdom of heaven, where nothing is impossible and resources are limitless.

In Psalm 78:9–11, Asaph writes: "The children of Ephraim, being armed and carrying bows, turned back in the day of battle. They did not keep the covenant of God; they refused to walk in his law, and forgot his works and his wonders that he had shown them."

Although they were armed and ready for battle, they turned back. Why? Bill Johnson comments: "The source of the problem was that they forgot the works and wonders of God. They failed to keep the testimony. When they failed to keep the testimony, they forgot who they were, who God was, and what He required of them."[8]

Bill Johnson continues, "Furthermore, consider this: Nearly every great leader of the Bible experienced the miraculous and/or supernatural—yet many Christians try to live without them. Exposure to the supernatural works of God changes the capacity of leaders to lead, thereby changing the bent of the people of God to pursue Him."[9]

Once Augustine started witnessing miracles of healing in his parish, he began to require people to give testimony of these healings, and he recorded those healings. John Wesley reported testimonies of the supernatural moves of God in peoples' lives in his *Arminian Magazine.* Such testimonies drew people to God and let them know that they were part of a group that expected to see God move supernaturally among them. They could expect God to move supernaturally in their own lives.

In the second church I served, we started a prayer room, largely following Terry Teykl's prayer room guidance.[10] And in that prayer room, we started a simple loose-leaf notebook that we called "The Deeds of God" book. In that book, people recorded answers to prayers that were prayed in the prayer room. It reflected ways that God was moving among us supernaturally.

Someone has said that if God were to withdraw His Holy Spirit from the world today, 95 percent of what we do in the church would continue without interruption. We are used to *not* experiencing the miraculous and/or the supernatural in our lives and in our churches. And we have become accustomed to operating without it.

Again, Bill Johnson writes, "The less we talk about the miraculous interventions of God, the lower our expectation to see them break out around us goes. The lower our expectation, the less we step into opportunities to minister to people. The less we minister to people, the less frequently we are exposed to the miracles of God around us. The less we're exposed to the miraculous, the less we talk about the miraculous…and the spiral can continue until eventually we lack any faith to see breakthrough in our circumstances, even when we've seen the very same impossibilities overcome by the power of God."[11]

I have included a list of scriptures in Appendix 6 that talk about the works of God and keeping the testimony. I encourage you to look them over and allow God to speak to you through them.

Having a rich supernatural church history and a Methodist supernatural history is not enough. As Bill Johnson cautions, "A supernatural history is easy for people to forget, especially when they want to feel good about themselves in the absence of miracles. When miracles are absent, and we are followers of Jesus, we instinctively want to create a reason why they are missing so we can live in our present state without making radical changes."[12]

Could this partially explain the rise of cessationism and dispensationalism? Miracles were absent, so the theological understanding that "God doesn't work that way in our day" would make cessationists feel comfortable with that.

In this book, I have traced some of the supernatural thread throughout the history of Methodism. Could it be that one of the reasons (not the only one) for the decline of Methodism in America is that American and Western-European Methodists, like the children of Ephraim, have largely forgotten the works and wonders of God done among the Methodists of the past?

In many of the places in the world where Methodism is growing, those Methodists are remembering the works and wonders of God in the past, and they are expecting them in the present. They are keeping the testimony. They are remembering who they are. And they are remembering who God is—a God of supernatural power, signs, wonders, and miracles.

We need Methodist leaders to lead in supernatural ministry. Bill Johnson counsels, "The responsibility of every leader in the church is to become exposed, and *remain* exposed, to the miracles of God and the God of miracles. Sincerity and genuine concern for the people of God are important but cannot take the place of such exposure. The transformation that takes place in and through the church because of the increase of supernatural activities does not happen just because spiritual leaders are reading some of the excellent books on Christian leadership. What is needed cannot be found through reading alone. It must come through exposure to the miracle realm. Nor will such a change happen by merely refining our leadership priorities to help bring out the best in others. Nothing can replace the transformation made possible through exposure to the glory of God through miracles. We owe it to those around us to do whatever is necessary to be impacted over and over again through God's miraculous activities on the earth. The rewards are priceless. The cost for this neglect is eternal."[13]

How will you provide opportunities for God to work supernaturally at your church? Start a prayer room. Have a special prayer time in worship or apart from worship where you specifically invite God to come and move supernaturally. Until miracles start happening at your church, go elsewhere to experience the miraculous, to places where they have been moving in the miraculous for a while. Don't leave your church! Go and bring that anointing back to your church. Get "exposed" so others in your church will be "exposed."

Bill Johnson's Bethel Church in Redding, California, is one such place. As he puts it, "Exposure is the key. When people who are truly born again become exposed to a genuine work of the Spirit of God, they suddenly rise to a purpose and call they never thought possible. This is the normal Christian life. And leaders who become exposed, *expose.* And so the nature of church life is changed."[14]

One of the main reasons that Aldersgate Renewal Ministries began the Methodist School for Supernatural Ministry was to expose pastors and church leaders to the miraculous so they would be changed and the nature of their church's life would be changed.

Most of us and most of our churches continue to restrict ourselves to a "life of the possible," as Bill Johnson calls it: "Without a sustained awareness of the God who invades the impossible, I will reduce ministry to what I can accomplish with my ministry gifts.... If we fail to regularly *remember* who God is, what He has done, and what he is going to do, we *will* make decisions on the basis of what we can accomplish without Him, which restricts us to a life of the 'possible.'"[15]

In his book *The Life of Reason,* George Santayana made that often-repeated statement: "Those who cannot remember the past are condemned to repeat it."[16] While that may be true for repeating the *mistakes* done in the past, it does not apply to the *good* things from the past. Those who will not remember and learn from the supernatural moves of God in the past *are not* destined to repeat them!

We need a new lens through which to view reality—a supernatural lens. We already know about the supernatural God of the Old Testament and the supernatural God of the Gospels and the Book of Acts. We need to see that that same God continued to do His work in church history, including among the Methodists, and that He is continuing to do His supernatural work among Methodists and others around the world today. Then we will know that He is able and willing to do His supernatural works through us! We need to develop our own history of the works of God in our own lives and the lives of our churches.

CONCLUSION

SHORTLY AFTER JOHN Wimber was converted, he read through the Bible and noticed how much of the Scriptures testify of our supernatural God moving in supernatural ways in this world and how God enabled His people to do His works. After he had attended a certain traditional church for several Sundays, he asked an usher, "When do you do the stuff?" The usher asked him, "What do you mean? What stuff are you talking about?" And Wimber replied, "You know, the signs and wonders and miracles of the Bible." The usher said, "We don't do that here!"

We don't do that here! Can that be said of your church? That should not be said of any United Methodist church, not with our history of the supernatural!

So, would you pray with me?

> Lord, we want to learn about the stuff, we want to see the stuff, and we want to do the stuff. We want to fully proclaim Your gospel by the power of signs and miracles, through the power of the Spirit. With the psalmist, we want to study, to seek after, to pursue Your works, O God. We want to pray for Your kingdom to come on earth as it is in heaven. We want Christ— the whole Christ, the supernatural Christ—to be formed in us. We want to do all the works that You had been doing.
>
> So, with the disciples in the Book of Acts (4:30–31) we pray that You would stretch out Your hand to heal and perform miraculous signs and wonders through the name of Your holy servant Jesus. We pray that You will shake this place where we are gathered and fill us all with Your Holy Spirit, that we might proclaim Your Word boldly with signs and wonders and miracles.

Appendix 1

RAISING THE DEAD IN SCRIPTURE AND HISTORY

By Dr. Frank Billman

But your dead will live; their bodies will rise. You who dwell in the dust, wake up and shout for joy. Your dew is like the dew of the morning; the earth will give birth to her dead.

—ISAIAH 26:19

WHEN THE APOSTLE Paul was before King Agrippa, he asked, "Why should any of you consider it incredible that God raises the dead?" (Acts 26:8) That is a good question for us today! Why should any of us consider it incredible that God raised the dead in the Bible, that God raised the dead in church history, and that God continues to raise the dead today? Christ gave orders to His apostles to raise the dead in Matthew 10:8. Why should we be surprised if some saints have followed those instructions?

Resuscitation is the divine miracle of restoring life to a person who has died. It is raising the dead back to a temporal life in the body, realizing that the person will eventually die again. The person is revived but still mortal. Resurrection is being raised to a glorified body that will never die again. The person is immortal. Lazarus experienced resuscitation. Jesus experienced resurrection, the first fruits of what Christian believers will experience (1 Cor. 6:14; 15:20). Paul calls death "the last enemy" in 1 Corinthians 15:26. Raising the dead is a demonstration that by the power of the Holy Spirit, even the last enemy cannot stand against the advancing kingdom of God.

129

REFERENCES TO RAISING THE DEAD IN SCRIPTURE

- 1 Kings 17:17–23—Son of the widow of Zarephath by Elijah

- 2 Kings 4:32–37—Shunammite's son by Elisha

- 2 Kings 13:21—Young man whose body touched Elisha's bones

- Luke 7:12–15—Widow's son at Nain by Jesus

- Luke 8:49–55—Jairus' daughter by Jesus

- John 11:43–44—Lazarus by Jesus

- Matthew 27:52—Dead raised in Jerusalem at death of Jesus

- Acts 9:37–40—Dorcas by Peter

- Acts 20:9–12—Eutychus by Paul

- Hebrews 6:1—Called an "elementary teaching"

- Hebrews 11:35—Women received back their dead

- Revelation 11:11—The Two Witnesses

SAINTS WHO RAISED THE DEAD IN CHURCH HISTORY

- Irenaeus (130–200)—reported it continuing frequently

- Macarius the Egyptian (300–380)

- Hilary of Poitiers (315–368)

- Martin of Tours (316–397)

- Ambrose (340–397)

- Augustine (354–430)—reported in his diocese

- Patrick of Ireland (389–461)—thirty-three raised from the dead

- Benedict (480–547)—he and his followers raised the dead

- Stanislas of Cracow (1030–1079)

- Bernard of Abbeville (1046–1117)

- Bernard of Clairvaux (1090–1153)

- Malachi of Ireland (1095–1148)

- Dominic (1170–1221)

- Ceslas (1184–1242)

- Hyacinth of Cracow (1185–1257)—fifty dead raised in Cracow alone

- Cyril (1191–1235)

- Anthony of Padua (1195–1231)

- Agnes of Prague (1205–1282)

- Berthold of Ratisbon (1220–1272)

- Herman of Gersthagen (1224–1287)

- Rose of Viterbo (1235–1252)—raised a dead person at three years old

- Jane of Signa (1244–1307)

- Agnes of Montepulciano (1268–1317)

- Margaret of Castello (1287–1320)

- Bridget of Sweden (1303–1373)

- Catherine of Sweden (1331–1381)—daughter of Bridget of Sweden

- Catherine of Siena (1347–1380)

- Vincent Ferrer (1350–1419)—at least thirty persons raised from the dead

- Angelina of Marsciano (1374–1435)

- Bernadino of Siena (1380–1444)

- Colette of Corbie (1381–1447)

- John Capistrano (1386–1456)

- Constantius of Fabrino (1410–1481)
- Joan of Arc (1412–1431)
- Mark of Modena (d. 1498)
- Francis of Paola (1416–1507)
- Colomba of Rieti (1468–1501)
- Ignatius of Loyola (1491–1556)
- Peter of Alcantara (1499–1562)
- Sebastian of Apparizo (1502–1600)
- Francis Xavier (1506–1552)
- Teresa of Avila (1515–1582)
- Felix of Cantalice (1515–1587)
- Vincent Bernedo of Lima (1562–1619)
- Giorcanni Eustachio of Larino (b. 1575)
- Marianne de Jesus of Quito (1618–1645)
- Francis of Jerome (1642–1716)
- Paul of the Cross (1694–1775)
- John (Don) Bosco (1815–1888)
- Billy Hibbard, an early American Methodist
- Smith Wigglesworth (1859–1947)
- John G. Lake (1870–1935)
- William Branham (1909–1965)
- Shantung Revival in China (1930s)

RAISING THE DEAD IN THE CHURCH TODAY

- Mel Tari in Indonesia
- David Hogan and others in Mexico—300+ raisings

- Surprise Sithole and pastors in Mozambique—400+ raisings
- James Rutz—In *Mega Shift,* the author gives accounts of raising the dead in fifty-two different countries around the world in 2005
- Dr. Chauncey Crandall—cardiologist in the US who raised a patient he had pronounced dead and God sent him back to pray for the patient
- Reinhard Bonnke in Nigeria—See YouTube
- Munday Martin in Tennessee

BIBLIOGRAPHY

Crandall, Chauncey. *Raising the Dead: A Doctor Encounters the Miraculous.* New York: Faith Words, 2010.

Crawford, Mary. *The Shantung Revival.* Originally published by China Baptist Publication Society, Shanghai, China, 1933. Current publication by Global Awakening, Mechanicsburg, PA, 2005.

Crowder, John. *Miracle Workers, Reformers, and the New Mystics.* Shippensburg, PA: Destiny Image, 2006.

Hebert, Albert J. *Saints Who Raised the Dead: True Stories of Four Hundred Resurrection Miracles.* Rockford, IL: Tan Books & Publishers, 1986.

Rutz, James. *Mega Shift: Igniting Spiritual Power.* Colorado Springs: Empowerment Press, 2005.

Tari, Mel. *Like a Mighty Wind.* New Leaf Publishing Group, 1991.

Appendix 2

A SHORT SKETCH OF THE LIFE AND CONVERSION AND CALL TO THE MINISTRY OF AUSTIN TAFT, MAY 10, 1887.

—*GOOD NEWS MAGAZINE*, SEPTEMBER/OCTOBER 1995, 26–27

MY PARENTS WERE Presbyterians after the strictest sect. We left Vermont when I was fifteen years old. I never saw but one Methodist in that state. We settled in the state of New York—Steuben Co., where I lived until I was married on the 9th of February 1831. Here I became acquainted with the people called Methodists. But I was taught they were from witches, full of wild fire and [that it] was dangerous to hear them preach. In 1833 we moved to Huron Co., Ohio. Here we found a Methodist Society that held their meetings in a log school house near our house.

We frequently went to hear them preach and I was convinced they enjoyed something that we knew nothing of. Subsequently a two-day prayer meeting was appointed in the neighborhood conducted by H. G. Dubois. We attended this meeting, but became offended at the loud and noisy demonstrations witnessed there and left with disgust.

The meeting continued and we were urged to come back by a good sister and attend the meeting; for the Lord was reviving His work. I told my wife it was none of their business whether we attended meeting or not—but if she desired to go I would harness the team and we would go.

We went and found a number of the leading men of the town at the altar of prayer pleading for mercy. I was invited to go and went and resolved that I would seek God until I found Him. With cries and tears, I pled for mercy. My feelings were so intense that I despaired even of life, but concluded I would spend life's last hour in pleading for mercy with little or no expectation of finding it. Eternity with all its dread realities opened up before me and it's impossible for any pen to describe the awful agonies of my mind. It is beyond all human description.

It seemed to me I had already entered the dark abodes of eternal night, and right here something seemed to whisper to me—that there was mercy for me. I stopped and listened for a moment. What a word—mercy for me. It was the best news I ever heard. From that moment my faith laid hold upon the Savior's promises with an unguiding grasp, and I saw a light in the distance far above my head, which grew brighter as it came near, and when it reached me I fell to the floor as quick as the lightning flash, and that moment was filled with the fullness of God. Old things passed away and all things became new. My happiness was complete....And I remained motionless for 45 minutes without power to move a muscle. My good Presbyterian father thought I was dead and talked of sending for the doctor.

The people were engaged in singing, shouting, and praising God—and it was the best music I ever heard. I arose singing "O How Happy Are They, Who Their Savior Obeyed." From that time to this I have never opposed the Methodists for making a little noise. I soon felt it my duty to join the Methodist Church; told my good mother one day at her house what my intention was. She told me not to do it; that it would be my ruin.

On my way home, while passing through a piece of woods, my heart was strangely drawn out in prayer. I fell upon my knees and asked God to send staying power upon my mother. That moment the power of God came upon me like a mighty rushing wind, and I know my prayer was answered. My sister came to our house that afternoon and said soon after I left their house while mother was setting the table for dinner she suddenly fell to the floor and shouted aloud the praises of God and thanked God that she had the same religion that Austin had. Father and mother soon joined the M.E. Church and have long since joined the church on high.

I felt from the time of my conversion that it was my duty to preach the Gospel of the Son of God. I told the Lord I had no education, had no gifts and it was impossible for me to preach. But I had no rest while I refused to do my duty.

At last I told the Lord if He would give an evidence that I could not doubt, I would try. I went into the dense forest about one-half mile and laid the case before God in prayer. And all at once the Savior appeared before me. There seemed to be a halo of Glory around His person, and His person appeared as bright as the lightning. This appearance was manifested twice and vanished out of sight but left inscribed upon the heavens in great bright golden capitals—The Promise—"Lo, I am with you always even unto the end of the world." O! How many hundreds of times have I realized the fulfillment of this blessed promise by feeling His presence with me when trying to speak for Him, and this is the best witness that we can have. Amen.

Appendix 3

A CYCLONE OF POWER AND GLORY IN ANSWER TO PRAYER

A T A CONVENTION of Christian workers, held in April 1882, we witnessed a spiritual cyclone. Forty or fifty ministers and laymen of different denominations had come together, for prayer and counsel, concerning the most important doctrines of the Christian church. Great differences of opinion were expressed, and the controversy became so sharp that some seemed offended, and the spiritual influence of the meeting sadly hindered. In fact, the powers of darkness threatened to come in like a flood, and overthrow the good that had already been done.

But some there were in that little company who knew the mighty power of prayer, and in that hour of need went on their faces before God with strong crying and tears. The Spirit interceded with groaning that could not be uttered, and soon an indescribably sacredness came over the meeting. A sister, who is in general opposed to what are termed outward manifestations, was so pressed in spirit that she began to groan aloud, and then to exclaim: "The Lord shall have His way! *The Lord shall have His way! The Lord shall have His way!*" Others began to weep. Then a minister who had come to the meeting strongly opposed to the views set forth by the leading workers, jumped to his feet, and shouted the praise of God, and began to tell of the mighty baptism of the Holy Ghost he had received. And sooner than we can write it, a veritable cyclone of God's power and glory swept over the place, carrying everything before it. Stubborn hearts yielded, and, in a very few moments of time, many were saved and filled with the Spirit.

Of this convention and closing service, a minister, who is now a presiding elder in the United Brethren Church, says: "The interest increased steadily from first to last, closing up in a tornado of Divine power. None who were present the last evening can ever forget how, at the first shout of victory, nearly all of the congregation rushed out of the house, only to return and gaze in speechless wonder, as souls being brought under conviction for sin, cried for pardon, or shouted their praises at being brought from nature's darkness to God's marvelous light. Others groaning under the conviction for holiness, wrestled until the carnal mind was cast out; when some leaped for joy, and others were laid prostrate under the weight of glory. Eternity alone can tell the blessed results of this closing service."[1]

THE METHODIST CHURCH AND THE CHARISMATIC MOVEMENT IN MALAYSIA

Approved by GCEC, 11–12 Aug 2006

THE HOLY SPIRIT AND REVIVAL

I. Introduction

A. Background and Purpose

The General Conference Executive Committee (GCEC) was presented with the issue that the ongoing influence of Pentecostal and charismatic churches and their practices has caused some problems for a number of Methodist churches, as well as some of our Annual Conferences. At the same time, it is recognized the renewed emphasis on the work of the Holy Spirit in the church has brought blessings to many as well. It was decided that a set of guidelines need to be drawn up for the whole Methodist Church so that this does not become a divisive issue, but one that would enhance our on-going ministry and mission instead.

This draft is based on the document, "The Methodist Church and the Charismatic Movement," which was officially approved by TRAC at its 9th Session in Nov. 1984 as a set of guidelines for TRAC churches. Much of the extraneous material has been removed and some additional material added. In drawing up the original report in 1984, much use was made of resource material already available, especially from the British Methodist Church and United Methodist Church (UMC). In fact the whole of Section III on "Guidelines" in the present draft is taken entirely from it the TRAC report, and that particular section of the TRAC report was taken with very minor changes from the UMC report.

B. *Defining Terms Used*

Terminology associated with the charismatic movement is confusing because of varying usage.

Pentecostalism: The term refers to the movement which began late in the 19th century in the Europe, and then later in the early 20th in USA, resulting in the formation of a number of Pentecostal denominations in the early years of the twentieth century. These include the Assemblies of God, Church of God, and the Foursquare Church. Classic Pentecostals in general assert that all must undergo the "baptism in the Holy Spirit," of which by speaking in tongues is the distinguishing mark. This experience is often subsequent to a Christian's conversion, the purpose of which is the empowering for ministry. In their view, Christians who have not undergone this experience are often considered to be at a lower spiritual plane than those who have been "baptized in the Spirit." Pentecostals also emphasize strongly the full recovery of the gifts of the Holy Spirit.

Charismatic Movement: This is the movement that began about 1960 in mainline Christian churches in the West, both Protestant and Roman Catholic, under the influence of the Pentecostal movement. Many, though not all, would follow classical Pentecostals in emphasizing the central importance of the baptism of the Holy Spirit, with the speaking in tongues as evidence. But all *Charismatics* would emphasize the need to recover the Holy Spirit's empowering and gifts for ministry today. Many emphasize the gifts of prophecy, healing, tongues, and interpretation of tongues because these gifts are perceived to have been neglected by the Church.

Charismatic: In popular usage the term *charismatic* is often associated with those in the *Charismatic movement* or *Pentecostal* churches as defined above. But in a biblical sense there is no such person as a "noncharismatic Christian," since the Greek term *charismata* refers to the gracious gifts of God bestowed upon all Christians to equip them for ministry: "to each is given the manifestation of the Spirit for the common good" (1 Cor. 12:7).

Indigenous Christianity: Pentecostals and *Charismatics* emerged out of Christianity in the West, where for long periods Christianity neglected the importance of the gifts of Holy Spirit in the life of the church. However, often when non-Westerners were converted, many of them read about the work of the Holy Spirit in the Bible and begin to practice them naturally. Examples of this include Sadhu Sundar Singh in India and John Sung in China. They were not *Pentecostals* or *Charismatics* in the Western sense, but they freely exercise the Holy Spirit's gifts. They are examples of *Indigenous Christianity*, i.e. forms of Christianity that emerged and grew under indigenous or local leadership in Asia, Africa, and Latin America.

II. Faith

A. Historical Perspective: The Work of the Holy Spirit in Various Periods

1. The Holy Spirit in the New Testament Period

The work of the Holy Spirit is clearly taught in the New Testament. The Lord Jesus was conceived by the Spirit (Luke 1:35), filled with the Spirit at His baptism (Luke 3:22), and empowered to face Satan at His temptation (Luke 4:1f). He claims to be the Spirit-filled Messiah foretold in the Old Testament who will come to bring God's salvation (Luke 4:18ff; 7:21f). His deliverance ministry of people in bondage to Satan was carried out in the Spirit's power (Matt. 12:28). And He will baptize with the Spirit and fire (Luke 3:15–19; John 7:37–39; 16:7; Acts 1:5, 8). Peter at Pentecost speaks of Jesus' "mighty works and wonders and signs that God did through him" (Acts 2:22).

The work of the Holy Spirit is clearly taught in the New Testament. The coming of the Spirit at Pentecost in Acts 2 ushered in the beginning of the church. It empowered the disciples to be witnesses of Jesus (Acts 1:8). The gifts of the Spirit are clearly taught (Rom. 12:6-8; 1 Cor. 12:4–11, 27–31; Eph 4:11; 1 Pet 4:10f). Paul describes his amazing missionary outreach to the Gentile world as "by word and deed, by the power of signs and wonders, by the power of the Spirit of God" (Rom. 15:18f).

2. The Holy Spirit in John Wesley's Life and Ministry

John Wesley and his followers were bearers of Scriptural Christianity and inheritors of the promises on the Holy Spirit in Acts and the rest of the New Testament. His own ministry and that of his followers testify to the dynamic work of the Spirit in early Methodism.

To begin with, his Aldersgate experience of the assurance of his salvation on 24th May 1738 was certainly a work of the Spirit. He relates how as he heard of "the change which God works in the heart through faith in Christ, I felt my heart strangely warmed...and an assurance was given that he had taken away my sins." Some months later, he was at prayer with seventy others, including his brother Charles and also George Whitefield, on the night of 1 Jan 1739. In the early hours of the next morning, the Holy Spirit was poured on them in a most powerful manner. He writes: "About three in the morning...the power of God came mightily upon us insomuch that many cried out for exceeding joy and many fell to the ground. As soon as we were recovered a little from that awe and amazement at the presence of His majesty, we broke out with one voice, 'We praise Thee, O God, we acknowledge Thee to be the Lord.'"

Careful study of Wesley's writings shows clearly that spiritual gifts, including healing and deliverance of the demonized, were clearly manifested in his ministry and that of his co-workers. There were also repeated cases of people falling to the ground under the power of the Holy Spirit due to a variety of reasons, including deliverance from demonization, deep conviction of sin and subsequent release, or simply being overcome by the Spirit (Davies, *Methodism*, pp. 60f; Heitzenrater, *Wesley and the People Called Methodists*, pp. 100f, 319). One study has shown that, "a careful study of Wesley's *Works* and particularly of the lives of the early Methodist preachers reveals evidence that all the spiritual gifts listed in 1 Cor. 12:8–10 were exercised, with the one exception of the interpretation of tongues" (Davies & Peart, *The Charismatic Movement and Methodism*, p. 2).

Finally, Wesley himself has noted that the spiritual gifts were not generally exercised after the first two or three centuries after Christ. But the reason for this was not that these gifts were not available. Rather, as he noted, "The real cause was 'the love of many,' almost all Christians, was 'waxed cold'" (cited in Snyder, 1982, p. 183).

3. The Pentecostal and Charismatic Movements in the West

Historically the roots of classical Pentecostalism in America are found in the 19th-century Holiness Movement, which in turn emerged out of Methodism. One writer, F. D. Bruner, rightly says that "Pentecostalism is Primitive Methodism's extended incarnation." Thus when Methodists evaluate the contemporary charismatic renewal, they are often touching their own deepest roots. In Europe, the roots were somewhat more varied, including Keswick holiness teaching and the Welsh Revival in Britain, and Pietistic teachings in Europe. The Charismatic Renewal in the West resulted from Pentecostal influence on the historic churches. Most of the major denominations were affected, including the Anglican, Baptist, Lutheran, Methodist, and Roman Catholic churches.

In the Malaysian context, many of the churches that are in these traditions are either from the classical Pentecostal traditions (mainly the Assemblies of God) or independent churches, which sprang up under the influence of Pentecostal and charismatic teachings, much of which have come from the West. But as it will be seen in the next section, there has also been significant indigenous input from Asian Christianity.

4. The Work of the Holy Spirit and Indigenous Christianity in Asia

However, the activity of the Holy Spirit is not merely restricted to Western Christianity. Indeed, when the gospel reached different parts of the non-Western world, especially Africa and Asia, many Christians learnt of the Holy Spirit's work in the Bible. In simple faith they believed, and many began exercising the gifts of the Spirit and saw "signs and wonders" in their ministries, just as it was in the New Testament. Although the ministries of such individuals and churches are similar those of Pentecostal and charismatic in many ways, they do not owe their origins to these Western. Rather, they sprang up entirely on their own under the direct leading of the Spirit.

Within Asia, the most famous examples would include people like

Sadhu Sundar Singh and Bahkt Singh in India, and Pastor Hsi (Sheng Mo) and John Sung (Shang-Jie) of China. These people operated freely in the realm of spiritual gifts such as visions and dreams, healings and exorcisms, prophecies and so forth. Further, whenever there have been deep-seated revivals in Asia, often there has been similar reports of the powerful work of the Spirit. These include the Mukti Mission revival in 1905 under the leadership of the most famous Indian woman Christian, Pandita Ramabai, the Indonesian revivals in the 1960s, and ongoing house-church revivals in China today.

5. SUMMARY

The above shows that work of the Holy Spirit in revival and the exercise of spiritual gifts is not something newly introduced by *Pentecostals* and *Charismatics* from the West. Rather, this is clearly taught in the New Testament and deeply rooted in our own Methodist tradition. Moreover, we see the same outpouring of the Spirit's power in some of the best and most dynamic examples of Asian Christianity. But it should also be noted that there have been aberrant movements which have caused unnecessary problems in the church.

B. Theological Perspectives

1. INTRODUCTION

We will now outline the basic theological position about the issues at hand. In deciding on the position we adopt, we must always allow Scripture and not our personal experience to guide us. There are three areas where clarification is needed. First, what does the phrase "baptism in/with the Spirit" mean and how is "tongues" related to it? Second, how should the experience of the work of the Holy Spirit affect church life, structures, and relationships? Thirdly, what should be our view of spiritual gifts? We shall look at each of this in turn.

2. Understanding "Baptism In/ by/With the Spirit"

A. All the Blessings of the Gospel Have Been Given in Christ

Every spiritual blessing has been given to us by God in and through our Lord Jesus Christ (Eph. 1:3), so that every Christian is complete, in principle, having received fullness of life in him (Col. 2:9, 10). This includes the gift of the Holy Spirit to all believers. The ministry of the Spirit is always to bear witness to and exalt Christ (Acts 1:8; John 16:8–15). Thus we must reject any idea that in the Spirit we receive something more wonderful than our Saviour, Jesus Christ, or something apart from Him and the fullness of His saving grace.

There is therefore the need (i) to avoid trying to stereotype either the work of the Holy Spirit or the experience of individual Christians into a one-, two- or three-stage experience; and (ii) to avoid presenting the work of the Spirit in separation from the work of the Son, since the Son gives the Spirit and the Spirit both witnesses to the Son and forms Him in us.

B. How Do We understand the "Baptism In/By/With the Spirit"?

Every Christian is indwelt by the Holy Spirit (Rom. 8:9). It is impossible for anyone to confess sin, acknowledge Christ as Lord, experience new birth, enjoy the Saviour's fellowship, be assured of being a child of God, grow in holiness, or exercise any faithful ministry without the Spirit. The Christian life is life in the Spirit. We all thank God for this gift.

In recent years there has been a fresh enrichment in many Christians' Spirit-given experience of Christ, and in many cases they have called it "baptism in/by/with the Holy Spirit." Some of these people have seen their experience as similar to that of the disciples on the Day of Pentecost, and other comparable events in Acts. Many people have used the phrase "baptism in/by/with one Spirit" in the *Pentecostal* sense of a post-conversion experience. Despite the observable parallels, however, there are problems attaching to the use of this term to describe an experience separated, often by a long period of time, from the person's initial conversion to Christ.

In the New Testament, this phrase occurs in the following places:

- 1 Cor. 12:13: "For we were all baptized in/by/with one Spirit into one body."
- Luke 3:16: "He will baptize you with the Holy Spirit and with fire."

If we begin with 1 Cor. 12:13, clearly the phrase "baptism in/by/with the Spirit" refers the experience of conversion and new birth, when a person is initiated into the body of Christ, i.e. the church. It has to be a once and for all event and applies to all Christians. In that sense, every person who has been saved by Christ, also has been baptized by the Spirit. It simply cannot be something that happens some time *after* conversion!

Concerning the usage of the word *baptism* in Luke 3:16, some scholars have pointed out that it is used in the sense of an overwhelming experience (cf. Mark 10:38; and Isa. 21:4 in Greek uses the same verb metaphorically of destruction). This would mean that Luke 3:16 refers to an experience wherein the Holy Spirit overwhelms us, including both emotionally and physically. If this is the case, then it would be similar to what the rest of the New Testament refers to as "being filled with the Spirit" (Acts 2:4; 4:31; 9:17f; Eph. 5:18).

It is difficult for all Christians to agree on using the phrase "baptism in/by/with the Spirit" in one standard way only, as it has been understood in different ways by different traditions. However, to avoid misunderstand among our own Methodist members, it is perhaps best to restrict the phrase to refer to the initial experience of the Spirit's coming into our lives at the moment of conversion and new birth. That is when we were "baptized" or immersed into the body of Christ, or incorporated into the church as a new Christian. At the same time, God desires to bless us ever more richly, both by strengthening us spiritually and morally so that we may become more and more like Christ, and also by empowering us for greater effectiveness in ministry. In the language of the New Testament, we can speak of this as "being filled with the Spirit." The advantage of this is that, as we are reminded in the New Testament, all of us need to be filled again and again. There are no exceptions!

c. How Do We Know That We Have Received the Gift of the Spirit or Been Filled With the Spirit?

Although speaking in tongues is an initial phenomenon recorded on a number of occasions in connection with receiving the Holy Spirit in the Book of Acts, the New Testament does not allow us to make it the only sure evidence that the Spirit has been given. Hence we must avoid at all cost saying to others that unless we can speak in tongues we have not been "baptized by the Spirit" or "filled with the Spirit." Indeed a careful study of 1 Cor. 12:28–30 shows that the Greek grammar in the question "Do all speak in tongues?" requires a firm "No." (At the same time it must be recognized that tongues is one of the spiritual gifts and its proper usage must not be discouraged.)

Nevertheless, it appears that the reception of the Spirit by Christians in the New Testament was something that was consciously experienced by the recipient, and often immediately perceived by onlookers (cf. Acts 8:18f; 19:2; Gal. 3:2). When we ask what evidence of this reception we might expect, in the light of the New Testament records, the immediate answer must be a new awareness of the love, forgiveness, and presence of God as our Father through Jesus Christ who is confessed as Lord, and the joyful spontaneous praise of God (whether in one's own tongue or another), issuing subsequently in a life of righteousness and obedience, and of loving service to God and man, a life which manifests gifts of the Spirit as well as spiritual understanding.

3. Church Life, Structures and Relationships

a. The Body of Christ

The New Testament teaches that the whole church is a charismatic community in which all are endowed with spiritual gifts (*charismata*) and are responsible for exercising them for the common good (1 Cor.

12:7). The rediscovery of spiritual gifts and doctrine of the body of Christ have helped in recent years to provide a healthy corrective to an earlier excessive individualism, wherein ministry in the church was centered primarily around the pastor. We welcome this and encourage every member to play a full part, through the exercise of his or her gifts in the life, worship, witness, and service of the church.

B. STRUCTURES

If the church is to benefit from these rediscovery of New Testament practices, traditional ways of worship, ministry, and congregational life must be modified and adapted. The doctrine and reality of the body of Christ cannot adequately be expressed through a pattern of ministry dependent chiefly, if not entirely, on one man. Neither can a rigid traditional "set" pattern of worship, which is sometimes found in our churches, fully express the freedom of the Spirit.

There is enough flexibility in our Methodist heritage at these points to allow for a genuinely corporate and Spirit-led church life. We there-fore urge all members to respect those traditions that are good and praiseworthy within Methodism on the one hand, and to be opened to the Spirit's leading on the other, as we seek to move forward in renewal.

c. THE MUTUAL ROLES OF PASTORS AND LAYPEOPLE

We believe a pastor must see himself as a trainer of others to be effec-tive members of the body of Christ. When members of a church are renewed and revived by the Spirit, they begin to exercise their gifts and to discover and develop their ministries. Lay leadership, therefore, begins to grow and mature. When that happens, the pastor's role in oversight, teaching, and leadership becomes more, not less, vital.

d. MAINTAINING UNITY AND PEACE IN CHURCHES

Often within a church there are those who are more traditional and those who have experienced the Spirit in a fresh way. There is place for mutual respect and acceptance, even when we disagree. We strongly urge that pastors and congregations pay careful attention to the guidelines in Section III so that the unity of the Spirit can always be maintained.

4. Spiritual Gifts

a. Their Nature, Range, and Variety

A spiritual gift is a God-given capacity to serve others in a manner that edifies them and helps them to know and love Christ more. Spiritual gifts are listed in Romans 12, 1 Corinthians 12, Ephesians 4 and 1 Peter 4. These list the most important and most commonly used gifts, but they are not exhaustive. Further, neither the context and terminology of 1 Corinthians 12 nor a comparison of the various lists of gifts will allow us to elevate one gift or set of gifts above another. And whilst not all gifts and ministries have been equally in evidence throughout the church's history, there is no reason why such gifts should not be given and exercised today. We should be open to receive any spiritual gifts that are consonant with the New Testament.

b. Gifts for Every Member

The New Testament teaches that every Christian has already received some gift or gifts, that all should recognize their gifts, and to exercise them. It also encourages all to desire further spiritual gifts of one sort or another, needed for ministry. The healthy functioning of a congregation as the body of Christ is dependent upon each one contributing in this way. We should therefore not be afraid to ask God for the needed gifts for the work He calls us to (Matt. 7:11).

c. Their Use, Regulation, and Oversight

We believe it is vital that those who claim to have gifts should have those gifts tested by the leadership in the body of Christ in that place, and not be given carte blanche to exercise them as if above being questioned or corrected. Christians with recognised gifts should not be stifled, but rather encouraged in their ministry by the leadership (1 Thess. 5:19–21). The exercise of gifts must be overseen by the eldership of the churches and by those more experienced in that field. Such gifts should normally be kept within the life of the whole church, and not restricted to some exclusive or special group.

5. Conclusion: The Goal of Renewal

The goal of renewal is not merely renewed individuals but a renewed and revived church, alive with the life of Christ, subject to the Word of God, filled with the Spirit, fulfilling Christ's ministry and mission, constrained by His love to preach the gospel, and enthralled in worship by the glory of Christ. Such a church alone can adequately portray Jesus Christ to the world. In preaching, writing, and counseling, the Christ-centeredness of the Christian life and the work of the Holy Spirit must constantly be emphasized, so that we may all together grow up fully into Him, our glorious Head.

III. Guidelines for Pastoral Practice

The following are a set of proposed "Guidelines" for all in the Methodist Church. (Note: In this section, the word *charismatic* will include both those who are charismatics in the Western sense and also those whose experience of the work of the Holy Spirit have come through indigenous Asian Christian sources.)

A. *Guidelines—The Local Church*

In facing the issues raised by charismatic experiences, we plead for a spirit of openness and love. We commend to the church the affirmations of 1 Cor. 13, as well as the classical ecumenical watchword: "In essentials, unity; in non-essentials, liberty; and, in all things, charity." Without an active, calm, objective, and loving understanding of the religious experience of others, however different from one's own, reconciliation is impossible.

The criteria by which we judge the validity of another's religious experience must include a compatibility with the mind and spirit of our Lord Jesus Christ, as revealed in the New Testament. If the consequence and quality of a reported encounter with the Holy Spirit give manifestations of division, self-righteousness, hostility, and exaggerated claims of knowledge and power, the experience is subject to serious question. However, when the experience clearly results in new dimensions of faith, joy, and blessings to others, we must conclude that this is what the Lord has done and offer him our praise.

1. Guidelines for All

a. Be open and accepting of those whose Christian experiences differ from your own.

b. Continually undergird and envelop all discussions, conferences, meetings, and persons in prayer.

c. Be open to new ways in which God by His Spirit may be speaking to the church.

d. Seek the gifts of the Spirit which enrich your life and you for ministry.

e. Recognize that, even though spiritual gifts may be abused, this does not mean that they should be prohibited.

f. Remember that the charismatic renewal has a valid contribution to make to the church.

g. Remember the lessons of church history when God's people rediscovered old truths; that the process is often disquieting; that it usually involves upheaval, change, and a degree of suffering and misunderstanding.

h. Always be mindful of the spiritual needs of the whole congregation.

i. In witnessing, teaching, or preaching, the wholeness of all aspects of the gospel must be presented.

j. Recognize the developments historically in the church's understanding of the work of the Holy Spirit and spiritual gifts so as not to repeat outdated controversies.

2. For Pastors Who Have Had Charismatic Experiences

a. Combine with your charismatic experience a thorough knowledge of, and an adherence to, Methodist policy and tradition. Remember your influence will, in large part, be earned by your loving and disciplined use of the gifts, by your conduct as a responsible pastor to all members of your congregation.

b. Seek a deepening and continued friendship with your clergy colleagues both within and without the charismatic experience.

c. Remember your ordination vows, particularly the vow to "maintain and set forward as much as lieth in you, quietness, peace, and love among all Christian people, and especially among those that shall be committed to your charge." Also, to "reverently" heed them to whom the charge over you is committed, following with a glad mind and will their godly admonitions.

d. Avoid temptation to force your personal views and experience on others. Seek to understand those whose spiritual experiences differ from your own.

e. Seek to grow in your skills as a biblical exegete, a systematic theologian, and a preacher in all the fullness of the gospel.

f. Pray for the gifts of the Spirit essential to your ministry; continually examine your life for the fruits of the Spirit.

g. Find significant expressions of your personal experience through ministries of social witness.

3. FOR PASTORS WHO HAVE NOT HAD CHARISMATIC EXPERIENCES

a. Continually examine your understanding of the doctrine and experience of the Holy Spirit and to communicate this with clarity.

b. Seek firsthand knowledge of what the charismatic renewal means to those who have experienced it. Keep your views open until this knowledge is obtained. Then observe and respond as a Christian, a Methodist minister, and as a sympathetic, conscientious pastor. Keep an openness to scriptural teaching regarding the charismatic gifts.

c. When speaking in tongues occurs, seek to understand its significance and relevance to the speaker.

d. Seek to know the meaning of the other "gifts of the Spirit" in the charismatic experience'utterance of wisdom, knowledge, the gift of faith, healing, miracles, and prophesying.

e. Methodist pastors should be intentional about the benefits to be derived by a mutual sharing of a variety of experiences which have biblical support.

Appendix 5

GUIDELINES: THE CHARISMATIC MOVEMENT AND THE UNITED METHODIST CHURCH

Approved by 2008 General Conference as number 8010 in the 2008 United Methodist Book of Resolutions *and number 8015 in the 2012* Book of Resolutions

INTRODUCTORY STATEMENT

I N 1976 GENERAL Conference approved "Guidelines: The United Methodist Church and the Charismatic Renewal." These "Guidelines" served the church well. At the 2004 General Conference, the GBOD was assigned the responsibility to review and revise the "Guidelines," while retaining their general focus and purpose.

GLOSSARY

Terminology associated with the charismatic movement is confusing because of varying usage.

Pentecostal refers to the movement whose roots began late in the nineteenth century, resulting in the formation of a number of Pentecostal denominations in the early years of the twentieth century. Classic Pentecostalism affirms what is sometimes spoken of as initial evidence, which includes the concept of requisite "baptism in the Holy Spirit" that every Christian must experience the "baptism in the Holy Spirit" that is accompanied by glossolalia or speaking in tongues as an "initial evidence." Pentecostals also emphasize strongly the full recovery of the gifts of the Holy Spirit.

Charismatic The word *charismatic* comes from the Greek word *charismata*, meaning "gifts." The root words in Greek mean "grace" and "joy." By definition, a charismatic should be a joyful, grace-gifted Christian. Charismatic Christians emphasize the need to recover the empowerment and the gifts of the Spirit for ministry today. They affirm the importance of all the "gifts of the Spirit."

Charismatic Movement Throughout this report the term *Charismatic Movement* is used to identify the movement that began about 1960 in mainline Christian bodies, both Protestant and Roman Catholic. This movement emphasizes the central importance of the "baptism of the Holy Spirit," but without the elevation of "speaking in tongues" as the initial evidence. A focus is placed on the need to recover the Holy Spirit's empowering and gifts for ministry today. These gifts include prophecy, healing, tongues, and interpretation of tongues, because these gifts are perceived to have been neglected by the church.

In a biblical sense there is no such person as a "non-charismatic Christian," since the term *charismata* refers to the gracious gifts of God bestowed upon all Christians to equip them for ministry: "To each is given the manifestation of the Spirit for the common good" (1 Cor. 12:7).

Pentecostals and Charismatics emerged out of Christianity in the West, where for long periods Christianity neglected the importance of the gifts of the Holy Spirit in the life of the church. However, the activity of the Holy Spirit is not merely restricted to Western Christianity. Indeed, when the gospel reached different parts of the non-Western world, many Christians learned of the Holy Spirit's work in the Bible. In simple faith they believed, and many began exercising the gifts of the Spirit. Although the ministries of such individuals and churches are similar to those of the Pentecostals and the charismatics in many ways, they do not owe their origins to these Western sources. Rather, they sprang up entirely on their own under the direct leading of the Spirit.

Neo-Charismatics, or *Third Wave* (the Pentecostals being the first wave and the charismatics being the second wave). These are Christians who, unrelated or no longer related to the Pentecostal or charismatic renewals, have become filled with the Spirit, energized by the Spirit, and exercise gifts of the Spirit without recognizing a baptism in the Spirit separate from conversion. Speaking in tongues is considered as optional or unnecessary. Signs and wonders, super-natural miracles, and power encounters are emphasized. Third-wavers form independent churches and do not identify themselves as either Pentecostals or charismatics (Synan, p. 396).

GUIDELINES

We believe the church needs to pray for a sensitivity to be aware of and to respond to manifestations of the Holy Spirit in our world today. We are not unmindful that the problems of discerning between the true and fraudulent are considerable, but we must not allow the prob-lems to paralyze our awareness of the Spirit's presence; nor should we permit our fear of the unknown and the unfamiliar to close our minds against being surprised by grace. We know the misuse of mys-tical experience is an ever-present possibility, but that is no reason to deny spiritual experiences.

In facing the issues raised by charismatic experiences, we plead for a spirit of openness and love. We commend to the attention of the church the affirmations of Paul on the importance of love in 1 Corinthians 13 and of Wesley: "In essentials, unity; in non-essentials, liberty; and, in all things, charity" (love that cares and understands). Without an active, calm, objective, and loving understanding of the religious experience of others, however different from one's own, har-mony is impossible.

The criteria by which we understand another's religious experience must include its compatibility with the mind and the spirit of our Lord Jesus Christ, as revealed in the New Testament. If the conse-quence and quality of a reported encounter with the Holy Spirit leads to self-righteousness, hostility, and exaggerated claims of knowledge and power, then the experience is subject to serious question. However, when the experience clearly results in new dimensions of love, faith, joy, and blessings to others, we must conclude that this is "what the Lord hath done" and offer God our praise. "You shall know them by their fruits" (Matt. 7:20).

GUIDELINES FOR ALL

1. Be open and accepting of those whose Christian experiences differ from your own.

2. Continually undergird and envelop all discussions, conferences, meetings, and persons in prayer.

3. Be open to new ways in which God by the Spirit may be speaking to the church.

4. Seek the gifts of the Spirit that enrich your life and your ministry, as well as the life of the church.

5. Recognize that although spiritual gifts may be abused in the same way that knowledge or wealth or power may be abused, this does not mean that they should be prohibited.

6. Remember that, like other movements in church history, the Charismatic Renewal has a valid contribution to make to the ecumenical church.

7. Remember the lessons of church history that when God's people rediscovered old truths the process was often disquieting and that it usually involved upheaval, change, and a degree of suffering and misunderstanding.

8. Always be mindful of the spiritual needs of the whole congregation.

9. In witnessing, teaching, or preaching, the wholeness of all aspects of the gospel must be presented.

FOR PASTORS WHO HAVE HAD CHARISMATIC EXPERIENCES

1. Continually examine your understanding of the doctrine and experience of the Holy Spirit, so you can communicate this with clarity.

2. Remember the lessons of church history when God's people rediscover old truths—the process is often disquieting, that it

usually involves upheaval, change, and a degree of suffering and misunderstanding.

3. Seek firsthand knowledge of what the Charismatic Renewal means to those who have experienced it. Keep your mind open until this firsthand knowledge is obtained. Then observe and respond as a loving Christian, as a United Methodist minister, and as a sympathetic, conscientious pastor. Keep to scriptural teaching regarding all the gifts of the Holy Spirit.

4. When speaking in tongues occurs, seek to understand what it means to the speaker in his/her private devotional life and what it means when used for intercessory prayer, especially in group worship.

5. Seek to understand the meaning of the other "gifts of the Spirit" in the charismatic experience, such as the utterance of wisdom, knowledge, faith, healing, miracles, and prophecy.

6. United Methodist pastors should be intentional about the benefits to be derived by a mutual sharing of a variety of experiences that have biblical foundation. Accordingly, the pastor should seek to keep all meetings called for prayer and fellowship open to all interested members of the congregation.

FOR PASTORS WHO HAVE NOT HAD CHARISMATIC EXPERIENCES

1. Continually examine your understanding of the doctrine and experience of the Holy Spirit so you can communicate this with clarity.

2. Remember the lessons of church history when God's people rediscover old truths: that the process is often disquieting, that it usually involves upheaval, change, and a degree of suffering and misunderstanding.

3. Seek firsthand knowledge of what the Charismatic Renewal means to those who have experienced it. Keep your judgments open until this firsthand knowledge is obtained (i.e., by attending and understanding their prayer meetings, etc.). Then observe and respond as a Christian, a United Methodist minister, and as a sympathetic, conscientious pastor. Keep an openness to scriptural teaching regarding the charismatic gifts.

4. When speaking in tongues occurs, seek to know what it means to the speaker in his or her private devotional life and what it means when used for intercessory prayer, especially in group worship. We should be aware that speaking in tongues is considered a minor "gift of the Spirit" by many who have charismatic experiences.

5. Seek to know the meaning of the other "gifts of the Spirit" in the charismatic experience, such as the utterance of wisdom, knowledge, the gift of faith, healing, miracles, or prophesying.

6. United Methodist pastors should be intentional about the benefits to be derived by a mutual sharing of a variety of experiences which have biblical support. Accordingly, the pastor should seek to keep all meetings called for prayer and fellowship open to all interested members of the congregation.

For Laity Who Have Had Charismatic Experiences

1. Remember to combine with your enthusiasm a thorough knowledge of and adherence to the United Methodist form of church government. The charismatic movement is closely related to the Holiness Movement and to the Wesleyan tradition. Consult with your pastor(s) and if they have not also had your experience, help him/her to understand what it means to you. Invite your pastor(s) to attend your worship services and prayer meetings.

2. Pray that the Spirit will help you to maintain fellowship with all United Methodists.

3. Strive for a scholarly knowledge of scriptural content in combination with your spiritual experiences. "Seek to unite knowledge and vital piety" (Wesley). Strive to integrate your experiences with the theological traditions of our church.

4. Avoid undisciplined, undiplomatic enthusiasm in your eagerness to share your experiences with others. Resist the temptation to pose as an authority on spiritual experiences. Failure in this area may cause your fellow Christians to interpret your behavior as spiritual pride.

5. Be intentional about keeping your prayer meetings and other gatherings open to all members of your congregation. When those who do not share your experiences do attend, discuss with them the purpose of the meeting with an interpretation of the significance of the content.

6. Remember that there are many types of Christian experiences that lead to spiritual growth; charismatic experience is one of these.

7. Accept opportunities to become personally involved in the work and mission of your own congregation. Let the results of your experience be seen in the outstanding quality of your church membership and service to others. Be an obvious, enthusiastic supporter of your congregation, its pastor, and its lay leadership and of your district, your annual conference, the General Conference, and mission of each. This may well be the most effective witness you can offer to the validity and vitality of your charismatic experience.

8. Remember Paul's injunction that when the gift of tongues is spoken to the body in a group context, there must be interpretation to ensure proper order (1 Cor. 14:27, 40). If the gift is exercised in a worship setting or group prayer, be careful that it does not hinder worship or cause distraction for others.

9. Keep your charismatic experience in perspective. No doubt it has caused you to feel that you are a better Christian. Remember that this does not mean you are better than other Christians but that you are, perhaps, a better Christian than you were before. Jesus commanded us to love one another (John 13:34).

For Laity Who Have Not Had Charismatic Experiences

1. We believe God is constantly seeking to renew the church, including the United Methodist Church. Pray that God may make known to you your own place in the process of renewal. The advent of the charismatic movement into our denomination is only one aspect of renewal.

2. If there are members of your congregation who have had charismatic experiences, accept them as brothers and sisters. Jesus commanded us to love one another (John 13:34).

3. Be aware of the tendency to separate ourselves from those who have experiences that differ from our own. Observe personally the charismatics in their prayer meetings, in your congregation, and in the mission of your church. Examine scriptural teaching about this. Pray about it. Discuss your concern with your pastor. The United Methodist Church is theologically diverse.

4. Do not be disturbed if your experience is not the same as others. The work and mission of a healthy congregation calls for many gifts (1 Corinthians 12–14). Each Christian is a unique member of the body of Christ and should seek to discover his/her gifts and role.

5. Should your pastor emphasize charismatic experiences, help her or him to be mindful of the spiritual needs of the entire congregation, to be a pastor and teacher to all. Encourage her or him in preaching to present the wholeness of all aspects of

the gospel. Be open to what God would say to you through your pastor about the Holy Spirit.

FOR CONNECTIONAL ADMINISTRATION

1. Refer prayerfully and thoughtfully to the other sections of these Guidelines.

2. Remember your pastoral responsibilities toward ordained persons and congregations within the connection, particularly toward those whose spiritual experience differ from your own.

3. Each administrator should consider whether any teaching or practice regarding the charismatic movement involving an ordained minister of a congregation is for the edification of the church.

4. If there is division involved in a particular situation, make as careful an evaluation as possible, remembering that there are other kinds of issues that may divide our fellowship—a lack of openness to something new or an unwillingness to change, for example. Sometimes tensions and conflicts may result in the edification and growth and maturity of the church and therefore need to be handled wisely and prayerfully by all concerned.

5. Administrators and connectional bodies will be required to deal with expressions of the charismatic movement. We urge all involved to seek firsthand information and experience about the movement, its meaning for those involved in it, and its value to the particular congregation.

6. Care should be taken that persons whose theology and experiences align with those of the Charismatic Renewal are not discriminated against in appointments or as candidates for ordination.

7. Where an ordained person seems to overemphasize or de-emphasize some charismatic doctrines/practices, she or he

should be counseled to preach the wholeness of the gospel, to minister to the needs of all of the congregation, and as a pastor to grow in understanding of our polity in the mission of the particular annual conference.

8. Annual conferences may also be faced with a situation where there is a charismatic group within a congregation whose pastor or whose lay leadership or both may be hostile to or ignorant of the charismatic movement. The Annual Conference Board of Ordained Ministry, the bishop, and the district superintendent have a pastoral responsibility to mediate and to guide in reconciliation, using these guidelines.

9. Pray continuously for sensitivity to the will and the leading of the Holy Spirit.

Guidelines reproduced from *Daily Christian Advocate,* April 27, 1976, vol. IV, no. 1, pp. 55–56.

HISTORICAL PERSPECTIVE

THE MINISTRY OF THE HOLY SPIRIT IN CHURCH HISTORY

The Holy Spirit in the New Testament Period

The Holy Spirit came upon Mary (Luke 1:35), descended upon Jesus at His baptism (Luke 3:22) and filled Jesus before the temptation in the wilderness (Luke 4:2ff). Jesus claimed that the Spirit was upon Him when he stood up to preach (Luke 4:18ff) and that the Spirit empowered Him to cast out demons (Matt. 12:28). John the Baptist and Jesus both indicated the importance of the power of the Spirit (Luke 3:15-19; John 7:37-39; Acts 1:5, 8).

The coming of the Holy Spirit ushered in the beginning of the church (Acts 2) and empowered the disciples to be witnesses (Acts 1:8, Acts 2:4ff). Paul writes about the gifts of the Spirit in his letters (Rom. 12:6-8; 1 Cor. 12:4-11, 27-31; Eph. 4:11) and describes his missionary outreach to the Gentiles as "by word and deed, by the power of signs and wonders, by the power of the Spirit of God" (Rom. 15:18ff; 1 Cor. 2:4-5; 1 Thess. 1:5).

The Holy Spirit in John Wesley's Life and Ministry

John Wesley and his followers were bearers of Scriptural Christianity. Their ministry testifies to the dynamic work of the Spirit in early Methodism.

To begin with, Wesley's Aldersgate experience of the assurance of his salvation on 24 May 1738 was certainly a work of the Spirit. He relates in his journal how as he heard of "the change which God works in the heart through faith in Christ, I felt my heart strangely warmed...and an assurance was given that he had taken away my sins." Some months later, he was at prayer with seventy others, including his brother Charles and also George Whitefield, on the night of 1 January 1739. In the early hours of the next morning, the Holy Spirit was poured on them in a most powerful manner. He writes: "About three in the morning...the power of God came mightily upon us insomuch that many cried out for exceeding joy and many fell to the ground. As soon as we were recovered a little from that awe and amazement at the presence of His majesty, we broke out with one voice, 'We praise Thee, O God, we acknowledge Thee to be the Lord.'"

"On the basis of Scripture, Wesley taught that the Holy Spirit is present and active in *every major stage of Christian experience*" (Stokes, 46). Careful study of Wesley's writings shows clearly that spiritual gifts, including healing and deliverance of the demonized, were clearly manifested in his ministry and that of his co-workers. There were also reported cases of people falling to the ground under the power of the Holy Spirit due to a variety of reasons, including deliverance from demonization, deep conviction of sin and subsequent release, or simply being overcome by the Spirit (Davies, *Methodism*, pp. 60f; Heitzenrater, *Wesley and the People Called Methodists*, pp. 100f, 319). One study has shown that, "a careful study of Wesley's *Works* and particularly of the lives of the early Methodist preachers reveals evidence that all the spiritual gifts listed in 1 Cor. 12:8–10 were exercised, with the one exception of the interpretation of tongues" (Davies and Peart, *The Charismatic Movement and Methodism*, 2).

Finally, Wesley himself has noted that the spiritual gifts were not generally exercised after the first two or three centuries after Christ. But the reason for this was not that these gifts were not available.

Rather, as he noted, "The real cause was 'the love of many,' almost all Christians, was 'waxed cold,' because the Christians were turned Heathens again, and had only a dead form left" (Sermon LXXXIX, "The More Excellent Way," *Works*, Vol. 7, 26–27). And Wesley wrote, "I do not recollect any scripture wherein we are taught that miracles were to be confined within the limits either of the apostolic or the Cyprianic age, or of any period of time, longer or shorter, even till the restitution of all things" ("Principles of a Methodist Farther Explained," *Works*, Vol. 8, 465).

THE PENTECOSTAL AND CHARISMATIC MOVEMENTS AND THE WESLEYAN FRAMEWORK

It is impossible to speak of Pentecostalism and the Charismatic Renewal apart from their roots in Methodism. It was, after all, the Wesleyans who first applied the title "pentecostal" to their movement and to a variety of their publications. The Methodists were also first to coin the phrase *baptism of the Holy Spirit* as applied to a second and sanctifying grace (experience) of God. (Cf. John Fletcher of Madeley, Methodism's earliest formal theologian.) The Methodists meant by their "baptism" something different from the Pentecostals, but the view that this is an experience of grace separate from and after salvation was the same. However, the roots of Pentecostalism in Methodist soil go much deeper than titles and phrases. While the phenomenon of speaking in tongues, commonly associated with Pentecostalism, was not an experience sought or promoted by early Methodists, other equally startling manifestations of the Spirit did abound. This was particularly so as Methodism spread across the American frontier. When asked once why the gifts of the Spirit, manifest in the early church, had disappeared, as if the church had no more need for them, Mr. Wesley responded: "It should not be reasoned that the absence of such in the church [eighteenth-century Church of England] reflects the reluctance of God to give, rather the reticence of the church to receive" (Tuttle, 106). Methodism then, at its inception, invited God's people to expect and receive whatever blessing God would give "for the common good" (1 Cor. 12:7). It is not surprising that many of the first Pentecostal leaders were originally Methodists. Pentecostalism has continued to be what Francis Asbury wanted Methodism to remain, a pliable movement more than a static institution. Whether Methodism claims it or not, Pentecostalism is an offspring and will perhaps be its greatest legacy. Conservative estimates of the number of classical denominational Pentecostals run 200 million. Combined with the millions of charismatics and neo-Pentecostals or third wavers and those in house churches, that number now stands at 500 million (Synan, 2) to 700 million (Rutz, 44–46), making this the second largest group of Christians in the world, second only to the Roman Catholic Church as a whole. This group is estimated to be growing worldwide by 8 percent a year (Rutz, 15).

Charismatics should interpret their gifts and experiences in light of their own traditions. When this does not occur, division and/or exploitation sets in. When United Methodist charismatics adopt a classical Pentecostal line, they are no longer United Methodist—at least in the Wesleyan sense. United Methodist charismatics need to recognize that, properly understood within the context of our own tradition, their charismatic gifts and experiences can be considered as fresh wind of the Spirit.

Wesley's theology of grace is in fact a theology of the Holy Spirit. He believed that Reformation theology was built upon the cardinal doctrine of original sin and that it is God's sovereign will to reverse our "sinful, devilish nature" by the work of the Holy Spirit. He called this activity of God prevenient, justifying, and sanctifying grace. Bound by sin and death, one experiences almost from the moment of conception the gentle wooing of the Holy Spirit—*prevenient grace*. This grace "prevents" one from wandering so far from God that when a person finally understands what it means to be a child of God the Holy Spirit enables us to say Yes to this relationship. For Wesley, this Yes was a heartfelt faith in the merit of Christ alone for salvation. It allows the Holy Spirit to take the righteousness that was in Christ and attribute or impute it to the believer—*justifying grace*. For Wesley this begins a *lifelong movement* from imputed to imparted righteousness in which the Holy Spirit moves the believer from the righteousness of Christ attributed through faith to the righteousness of Christ realized within the individual—*sanctifying grace*.

To understand Wesley's experience of "entire sanctification" is to know how far the Pentecostal baptism of the Holy Spirit falls short if there are not continuing works of grace. Grace is continual, though we may not always perceive it. It is essential that we do not confuse being "filled with the Holy Spirit" with Wesley's mature doctrine of sanctification. The Spirit-filled life is, rather, a sustained journey of gifts, experiences, and divine support, beginning with conversion, constantly moving us toward the goal of sanctification.

Many charismatics have come to believe that being filled with the Holy Spirit is an experience that begins with justification and continues as a lifelong process of growth in grace. For the charismatic, Spirit-baptism bestows not one but many gifts and not one but many experiences intended to sustain one day after day. Being baptized in the Spirit (Acts 1:4–5) and being continually filled with the Spirit (Eph. 5:18) and walking with the Spirit (Gal. 5:25) are important parts of the *journey* toward Christ-likeness, but they are only *parts* of the journey. Thus, United Methodist charismatics, within the context of our own rich tradition, can never interpret gifts and experiences as signs of superior spirituality, making them better than others. Rather, the power of God being sustained within them makes them better than they were and able "to press on toward the goal for the prize of the heavenly call of God in Christ Jesus" (Phil. 3:14).

The Charismatic Renewal has been instrumental in providing many gifts to the Church of Christ Jesus and has made a profound impact upon present-day United Methodism.

Methodists throughout history have always worshipped God in a variety of styles—never more so than today. In addition worship itself—from openly free to highly liturgical—is now more broadly and correctly understood as a personal offering from the body rather than simply the service of worship that one attends. "God is spirit, and those who worship him, must worship in spirit and truth" (John 4:24).

Contemporary Christian music—a hallmark of the charismatic renewal—fills many of our churches each Sunday, enriches the spiritual life of individuals, and enhances small group meetings.

There are a variety of healing services offered in *The United Methodist Book of Worship*. In addition, the church offers a number of helpful resources for beginning and sustaining healing ministries within the local church.

Spiritual formation is now considered an integral part of planning for annual conferences and important in the continuing education for clergy.

The renewing work of the Holy Spirit within the United Methodist Church has supported the Lay Witness Movement, the Walk to Emmaus, and the Academy for Spiritual Formation. In 1978, Aldersgate Renewal Ministries (whose purpose is to "encourage United Methodists to be filled, gifted, empowered and led by the Holy Spirit in ministry to the world") became an affiliate of the General Board of Discipleship. These ministries have been used by God to bring thousands of people around the world into a new or deeper relationship with the Lord.

United Methodist charismatics and non-charismatics alike should be encouraged. In fact, the term *non-charismatic* Christian is a misnomer. All Christians have gifts. *Charismatic,* as earlier defined, refers to those who more explicitly acknowledge and emphasize teaching concerning the power of the Holy Spirit at work within them and the church through such gifts.

BOOKS AND PERIODICALS FOR
THE GENERAL READER

Davies, Rupert E. *Methodism*. London: Epworth, 1976. This is a standard reference work written by a British Methodist scholar.

Davies, William R. and Peart, Ross. *The Charismatic Movement and Methodism*. Westminster, UK: Methodist Home Mission, 1973. This resource written by clergy within the charismatic tradition of the British Methodist Church.

DeArteaga, William. *Quenching the Spirit: Discover the Real Spirit Behind the Charismatic Controversy*. Lake Mary, FL: Creation House, 2002. This volume contains a historical overview of spiritual gifts from the early church to the date of publication. It also provides the history of opposition to spiritual gifts. www .creationhouse.com.

Heitzenrater, Richard P. *Wesley and the People Called Methodists*.

Nashville: Abindgdon, 1995. This is a standard reference work written by a United Methodist scholar in the USA. www.cokesbury.com.

"The Holy Spirit and Revival." The Methodist Church in Malaysia. August 2006. This document was recently approved in Malaysia and represents a more global and biblical perspective on spiritual gifts.

Hyatt, Eddie L. *2000 Years of Charismatic Christianity.* Lake Mary, FL: Charisma House, 2002. This book traces the history of charismatic Christianity from the early church to the present time with significant attention to Methodism. www.charismahouse.com.

Jennings, Daniel R. *The Supernatural Occurrences of John Wesley.* Sean Multimedia, 2005. This resource gathers information from John Wesley's writings on spiritual gifts and the supernatural. www.seanmultimedia.com.

Moore, Gary L. *Life in the Spirit Seminar.* Franklin, TN: Providence House, 2003. This resource is the manual for local church Life in the Spirit seminars. It also can be used for small group Bible studies on the Holy Spirit from a Wesleyan perspective. www.aldersgaterenewal.org.

Rutz, James. *Mega Shift.* Colorado Springs: Empowerment Press, 2005. This resource describes the miraculous work of God around the world through ordinary people and the house-church movement.

Stokes, Mack B. *The Holy Spirit in the Wesleyan Heritage.* Nashville: Abingdon Press, 1985, 1993. This is a standard work by a bishop of the United Methodist Church.

Synan, Vinson. *The Century of the Holy Spirit: 100 Years of Pentecostal and Charismatic Renewal.* Nashville: Thomas Nelson, 2001. This book traces the development of the Pentecostal, Charismatic, and Third Wave movements from 1901–2001, including references to Methodism.

Tuttle, Robert G. *Sanctity Without Starch.* Anderson, IN: Bristol Books, 1992. A standard work by a United Methodist theologian within the charismatic tradition.

Appendix 6

SCRIPTURES ON THE TESTIMONIES
AND WORKS OF GOD

(from the New King James Version)

For He established a testimony in Jacob, and appointed a law in Israel, which He commanded our fathers, that they should make them known to their children; that the generation to come might know them, the children who would be born, that they may arise and declare them to their children, that they may set their hope in God, and not forget the works of God, but keep his commandments.

—Psalm 78:5–7

They still sinned, and did not believe in His wondrous works.... They tempted God, and limited the Holy One of Israel.

—vv. 32, 41

They did not remember His power: the day when He redeemed them from the enemy, when He worked His signs in Egypt, and His wonders in the field of Zoan....Yet they tested and provoked the Most High God, and did not keep His testimonies.

—vv. 42–43, 56

Oh, give thanks to the LORD! Call upon His name; make known His deeds among the peoples! Sing to Him, sing psalms to Him; talk of all His wondrous works!...Remember His marvelous works which He has done, His wonders, and the judgments of His mouth....Declare His glory among the nations, His wonders among all peoples.

—1 Chronicles 16:8–9, 12, 24

I will praise You, O Lord, with my whole heart; I will tell of all Your marvelous works.

—Psalm 9:1

That I may proclaim with the voice of thanksgiving, and tell of all Your wondrous works.

—Psalm 26:7

Because they do not regard the works of the Lord, nor the operation of His hands, He shall destroy them and not build them up.

—Psalm 28:5

Many, O Lord my God, are Your wonderful works which You have done; and Your thoughts toward us cannot be recounted to You in order; if I would declare and speak of them, they are more than can be numbered.

—Psalm 40:5

Come, behold the works of the Lord.

—Psalm 46:8

All men shall fear, and shall declare the work of God; for they shall wisely consider His doing.

—Psalm 64:9

Say to God, "How awesome are Your works! Through the greatness of Your power Your enemies shall submit themselves to You."...Come and see the works of God; He is awesome in His doing toward the sons of men.

—Psalm 66:3, 5

O God, You have taught me from my youth; and to this day I declare Your wondrous works. Now also when I am old and grayheaded, O God, do not forsake me, until I declare Your strength to this generation, your power to everyone who is to come.

—Psalm 71:17–18

But it is good for me to draw near to God; I have put my trust in the Lord God, that I may declare all Your works.

—Psalm 73:28

We give thanks to You, O God, we give thanks! For Your wondrous works declare that Your name is near.

—Psalm 75:1

And I said, "This is my anguish; But I will remember the years of the right hand of the Most High." I will remember the works of the Lord; surely I will remember Your wonders of old. I will also meditate on all Your work, and talk of Your deeds.

—Psalm 77:10–12

Among the gods there is none like You, O Lord; nor are there any works like Your works. All nations whom You have made shall come and worship before You, O Lord, and shall glorify Your name. For You are great, and do wondrous things; You alone are God.

—Psalm 86:8–10

For You, Lord, have made me glad through Your work; I will triumph in the works of Your hands. O Lord, how great are Your works!

—Psalm 92:4–5

Oh, give thanks to the Lord! Call upon His name; make known His deeds among the peoples! Sing to Him, sing psalms to Him; talk of all his wondrous works!... Remember His marvelous works which He has done, His wonders, and the judgments of His mouth.

—Psalm 105:1–2, 5

Who can utter the mighty acts of the Lord?... Our fathers in Egypt did not understand Your wonders.... They soon forgot His works.... They forgot God their Savior, who had done great things in Egypt, wondrous works in the land of Ham.

—Psalm 106:2, 7, 13, 21–22

Oh, that men would give thanks to the Lord for His goodness, and for His wonderful works to the children of men!

—Psalm 107:8, 15, 21, 31

The works of the LORD are great, studied by all who have pleasure in them.... He has made His wonderful works to be remembered.... He has declared to His people the power of His works.

—PSALM 111:2, 4, 6

I shall not die, but live, and declare the works of the LORD.

—PSALM 118:17

Make me understand the way of Your precepts; so shall I meditate on Your wonderful works.

—PSALM 119:27

Do not forsake the works of Your hands.

—PSALM 138:8

I remember the days of old; I meditate on all Your works; I muse on the work of Your hands.

—PSALM 143:5

One generation shall praise Your works to another, and shall declare Your mighty acts. I will meditate on the glorious splendor of your majesty, and on Your wondrous works. Men shall speak of the might of Your awesome acts, and I will declare Your greatness. They shall utter the memory of Your great goodness, and shall sing of Your righteousness.... All Your works shall praise You, O LORD, and Your saints shall bless You. They shall speak of the glory of Your kingdom, and talk of Your power, to make known to the sons of men His mighty acts, and the glorious majesty of His kingdom.

—PSALM 145:4–7, 10–12

But they do not regard the work of the LORD, nor consider the operation of His hands. Therefore my people have gone into captivity, because they have no knowledge.

—ISAIAH 5:12–13

Therefore, behold, I will again do a marvelous work among this people, a marvelous work and a wonder.

—ISAIAH 29:14

"Perhaps the LORD will deal with us according to all His wonderful works, that the king may go away from us."

—JEREMIAH 21:2

"What shall we do, that we may work the works of God?"

—JOHN 6:28

These are the testimonies, the statutes, and the judgments which Moses spoke to the children of Israel after they came out of Egypt.

—DEUTERONOMY 4:45

You shall diligently keep the commandments of the LORD your God, His testimonies, and His statutes which He has commanded you.... When your son asks you in time to come, saying, "What is the meaning of the testimonies, the statutes, and the judgments which the LORD our God has commanded you?" then you shall say to your son: "We were slaves of Pharaoh in Egypt, and the LORD brought us out of Egypt with a mighty hand; and the LORD showed signs and wonders before our eyes, great and severe, against Egypt, Pharaoh, and all his household."

—DEUTERONOMY 6:17, 20–22

"Keeping God's testimonies."

—1 KINGS 2:3; 2 KINGS 23:3; 1 CHRONICLES 29:19; 2 CHRONICLES 34:31; PSALM 25:10; 78:56; 99:7; 119:2, 22, 146, 167, 168

Your testimonies are very sure.

—PSALM 93:5

I have rejoiced in the way of Your testimonies, as much as in all riches.... Your testimonies also are my delight and my counselors.... I cling to your testimonies.... Incline my heart to Your testimonies.... I will speak of your testimonies also before kings, and will not be ashamed.... I thought about my ways, and turned my feet to Your testimonies.... Let those who fear You turn to me, those who know Your testimonies.... The wicked wait for me to destroy me, but I will consider Your testimonies.... I have more understanding than all my teachers, for Your testimonies are my meditation.... Your testimonies I have taken as a heritage forever, for they are the rejoicing of my heart.... Therefore I love Your testimonies.... I am Your servant; give me understanding, that I may know Your testimonies.... Your testimonies are wonderful; therefore my soul keeps them.... Your testimonies, which You have commanded, are righteous and very faithful.... The righteousness of Your testimonies is everlasting; give me understanding, and I shall live.... Concerning your testimonies, I have known of old that You have founded them forever.... Many are my persecutors and my enemies, yet I do not turn from Your testimonies.

—PSALM 119:14, 24, 31, 36, 46, 59, 79, 95, 99, 111, 119, 125, 129, 138, 144, 152, 157

"Because...you have not obeyed the voice of the LORD or walked in His law, in His statues or in His testimonies, therefore this calamity has happened to you, as at this day."

—JEREMIAH 44:23

BIBLIOGRAPHY

Arnott, John G. *The Father's Blessing.* St. Mary, FL: Charisma Media, 1996.

Badley, Brenton T. *Warne of India: The Life-Story of Bishop Francis Wesley Warne.* Madras, India: Madras Publishing House, 1932.

Beard, Steve. *Thunderstruck: John Wesley and the Toronto Blessing.* Wilmore, KY: Thunderstruck Communications, 1996.

Brawley, Vince. "The Lady From Baga." *Mission Society News.* August 25, 2011.

Case, Riley. "Cutting out Options for Seminary Education." *We Confess* (March/April, 2007).

Chilcote, Paul Wesley. *Her Own Story: Autobiographical Portraits of Early Methodist Women.* Nashville: Kingswood Books, 2001.

Clark, Randy. *Evangelism Unleashed.* Mechanicsburg, PA: Global Awakening, 2005.

———, comp. *Supernatural Missions: The Impact of the Supernatural on World Missions.* Mechanicsburg, PA: Global Awakening, 2012.

———. *There Is More! Reclaiming the Power of Impartation.* Mechanicsburg, PA: Global Awakening, 2006.

Crandall, Chauncey. *Raising the Dead: A Doctor Encounters the Miraculous.* New York: Faith Words, 2010.

Crawford, Mary. *The Shantung Revival.* Shanghai, China: China Baptist Publication Society, 1933. Reprinted by Global Awakening, Mechanicsburg, PA, 2005.

Crowder, John. *The Ecstasy of Loving God: Trances, Raptures, and the Supernatural Pleasures of Jesus Christ.* Shippensburg, PA: Destiny Image, 2009.

———. *Miracle Workers, Reformers, and the New Mystics: How to*

Become Part of the Supernatural Generation. Shippensburg, PA: Destiny Image, 2006.

Dallimore, Arnold A. *George Whitefield.* London: The Banner of Truth Trust, 1970.

Daniels, W. H. *The Illustrated History of Methodism in Great Britain and America, From the Days of the Wesleys to the Present Time.* New York: Philips & Hunt, 1880.

Davies, Larry. www.sowingseedsoffaith.com. February 26, 2012.

DeArteaga, William. *Quenching the Spirit: Discover the Real Spirit Behind the Charismatic Controversy.* Lake Mary, FL: Creation House, 1996.

DeCenso Jr., Frank, ed. *God's Supernatural Power in You.* Shippensburg, PA: Destiny Image, 2009.

Ferguson, Charles W. *Organizing to Beat the Devil: Methodists and the Making of America.* Garden City, NY: Doubleday & Company, 1971.

Galli, Mark. "Revival at Cane Ridge." *Christian History* 45 (vol. XIV, no. 1).

Hebert, Albert. J. *Saints Who Raised the Dead: True Stories of Four Hundred Resurrection Miracles.* Rockford, IL: Tan Books and Publishers, 1986.

Hyatt, Eddie. *2000 Years of Charismatic Christianity.* Lake Mary, FL: Charisma House, 2002.

Jennings, Daniel. *The Supernatural Occurrences of John Wesley.* Sean Multimedia, 2005.

Johnson, Bill. *Release the Power of Jesus.* Shippensburg, PA: Destiny Image Publishers, 2009.

Keener, Craig S. *Miracles: The Credibility of the New Testament Accounts.* Grand Rapids: Baker Academic, 2001.

Liardon, Roberts. *The Azuza Street Revival: When the Fire Fell.* Shippensburg, PA: Destiny Image Publishers, 2006.

———. *God's Generals: Why They Succeeded and Why Some Failed.* New Kensington, PA: Whitaker House, 1996.

Lunn, Arnold. *John Wesley.* New York: The Dial Press, 1929.

MacMullen, Ramsay. *Christianizing the Roman Empire (A.D. 100–400)*. New Haven, CT: Yale University Press, 1984.

MacNutt, Francis. *The Healing Reawakening: Reclaiming Our Lost Inheritance*. Grand Rapids: Chosen Books, 2005.

———. *Overcome by the Spirit*. Grand Rapids: Chosen Books, 1990.

Oconer, Luther J. "The *Culto Pentecostal* Story: Holiness Revivalism and the Making of Philippine Methodist Identity, 1899–1965." Dissertation. Madison, NJ: Drew University, 2009.

———. "Methodism in Asia and the Pacific." In *T & T Clark Companion to Methodism*, Charles Yrigoyen, Jr. ed. New York: T & T Clark International, 2010.

O'Malley, J. Steven & Jason E. Vickers, eds. *Methodist and Pietist: Retrieving the Evangelical United Brethren Tradition*. Nashville: Kingswood Books, 2011.

Porter, James. *Compendium of Methodism*. 11th ed. Boston: George C. Rand, 1856.

Reeves, Martin. "God Knows Our Needs: Unborn Baby Is Healed." *Mission Society Newsletter* (September 2012).

Riss, Richard M. *A Survey of Twentieth-Century Revival Movements in North America*. Peabody, MA: Hendrickson Press, 1988.

Ruth, Lester. *Early Methodist Life and Spirituality: A Reader*. Kingswood Books: Nashville, TN, 2005.

———. *A Little Heaven Below: Worship at Early Methodist Quarterly Meetings*. Kingswood Books: Nashville, TN, 2000.

Rutz, James. *Mega Shift: The Best News Since Year One*. Colorado Springs: Empowerment Press, 2005.

Schmidt, Leigh Eric. *Holy Fairs: Scotland and the Making of American Revivalism*. 2d edition. Grand Rapids: Eerdmans, 2001.

Schmitt, Charles P. *Floods Upon the Dry Ground*. Shippensburg, PA: Destiny Image, 1998.

Scott, James B. & Molly Davis. *Restoring Methodism: Ten Decisions for United Methodist Churches in America*. Dallas: Provident Publishing, 2006.

Shaw, Solomon B.. *Touching Incidents and Remarkable Answers to*

Prayer. Lansing, Mich.: J. W. Hazleton, 1893, public doman. Reprinted by www.general-books.net, 2009.

"Should We Expect a Miracle?" *Mission Society Newsletter* (September 2012).

Synan, Vinson. *The Century of the Holy Spirit: 100 Years of Pentecostal and Charismatic Renewal*. Nashville: Thomas Nelson, 2001.

———. *The Holiness-Pentecostal Movement*. Grand Rapids: Eerdmans, 1971.

———. ed. *The Twentieth-Century Pentecostal Explosion: The Exciting Growth of Pentecostal Churches and Charismatic Renewal Movements*. Altamonte Springs, FL: Creation House, 1987.

Talbot, Michael. *The Holographic Universe*. New York: Harper Collins, 1991.

Taves, Ann. *Fits, Trances, and Visions: Experiencing Religion and Explaining Experience From Wesley to James*. Princeton, NJ: Princeton University Press, 1999. Quoted passages reprinted by permission of Princeton University Press.

Teykl, Terry. *Making Room to Pray: How to Start and Maintain a Prayer Room in Your Church*. Muncie, IN: Prayer Point Press, 1993.

The Sentinel Group. *Appalachian Dawn*. DVD. www.sentinelgroup.org, 2010.

———. *Let the Sea Resound*. DVD. www.sentinelgroup.org, 2004.

Wagner, James. *An Adventure in Healing and Wholeness: The Healing Ministry of Christ in the Church Today* . Nashville: Upper Room Books, 1993.

———. *Blessed to Be a Blessing*. Nashville: Upper Room Books, 1980.

———. *Healing Services*. Nashville: Abingdon Press, 2007.

Waugh, Geoff. *Revival Fires*. Mechanicsburg, PA: Global Awakening, 2009.

Wesley, John. *The Works of John Wesley*. 3d edition. 14 Volumes. Grand Rapids: Baker Books, 1996.

White, John. *When the Spirit Comes With Power: Signs and Wonders Among God's People*. Downers Grove, IL: Inter Varsity Press, 1988.

Wigger, John. "Holy, 'Knock-'Em-Down' Preachers." *Christian History* 45 (vol. XIV, no. 1).

———. *Taking Heaven by Storm: Methodism and the Rise of Popular Christianity in America*. Chicago: University of Illinois Press, 1998.

Wood, Laurence W. *The Meaning of Pentecost in Early Methodism: Rediscovering John Fletcher as John Wesley's Vindicator and Designated Successor*. Lantham, MD: Scarecrow Press, 2002.

Wright, Fred and Sharon. *The World's Greatest Revivals*. Shippensburg, PA: Destiny Image, 2007.

Yung, Hwa. "A 21st-Century Reformation: Recover the Supernatural." *Christianity Today* (September 11, 2010).

NOTES

CHAPTER ONE
SUPERNATURAL MANIFESTATIONS IN CHURCH HISTORY

1. John Wesley, *The Works of John Wesley*, X, "Letter to the Rev. Dr. Middleton," 21.

2. Ibid.

3. Ibid., 22.

4. Ibid.

5. Wesley, *The Works of John Wesley*, II, *Journal*, August 15, 1740, 204.

6. Francis MacNutt, *The Healing Reawakening* (Grand Rapids, MI: Chosen Books, 2005), 80.

7. Ibid., 81.

8. Ibid., 83.

9. Wesley, "Letter to the Rev. Dr. Middleton," 22–23.

10. Ibid., 23.

11. Quoted in MacNutt, *Healing Reawakening*, 83.

12. Ibid., 81.

13. William DeArteaga, *Quenching the Spirit* (Lake Mary, FL: Creation House, 1996), 64.

14. Ibid., 65.

15. Ibid.

16. Ibid., 66.

17. Ibid., 66–67.

18. John Crowder, *Miracle Workers, Reformers, and the New Mystics* (Shippensburg, PA: Destiny Image, 2006), 67.

19. DeArteaga, *Quenching*, 67.

20. Ibid., 79.

21. Ibid., 67.

22. Quoted in Charles Schmitt, *Floods Upon the Dry Ground* (Shippensburg, PA: Revival Press, 1998), 56–57.

23. MacNutt, *Healing Reawakening*, 111–112.

24. Ibid., 112.

25. DeArteaga, *Quenching*, 71.

26. Ibid., 72–73.

27. Ibid., 73.

28. Quoted in MacNutt, *Healing Reawakening*, 115.

29. Eddie Hyatt, *2000 Years of Charismatic Christianity* (Lake Mary, FL: Charisma House, 2002), 44–45.

30. Fred and Sharon Wright, *The World's Greatest Revivals* (Shippensburg, PA: Destiny Image, 2007), 86.

31. Quoted in Charles P. Schmitt, *Floods*, 67–68.

32. Wright, *Revivals*, 87.

33. Richard Riss, *A Survey of Twentieth-Century Revival Movements in North America* (Peabody, MA: Hendrickson Publishers, 1988), 8.

34. Schmitt, *Floods*, 81.

35. Crowder, *New Mystics*, 167.

36. Ibid., 168.

37. Hyatt, *2000 Years*, 55.

38. Schmitt, *Floods*, 72.

39. MacNutt, *Healing Reawakening*, 129.

40. Crowder, *New Mystics*, 172.

41. Schmitt, *Floods*, 71.

42. Wright, *Revivals*, 87.

43. MacNutt, *Healing Reawakening*, 157.

44. Ibid., 158.

45. Wright, *Revivals*, 87.

46. Schmitt, *Floods*, 73.

47. Riss, *Twentieth Century*, 9.

48. MacNutt, *Healing Reawakening*, 158.

49. Ibid., 133.

50. Ibid., 134.

51. Ibid., 135.

52. Ibid., 136.

53. Ibid., 137.

54. Albert Hebert, *Saints Who Raised the Dead* (Rockford, IL: Tan Books & Publishers, 1986).

55. MacNutt, *Healing Reawakening*, 126.

56. Ibid., 124.

57. Ibid., 127.

58. Ibid., 129.

59. DeArteaga, *Quenching*, 38.

60. John Crowder, *The Ecstasy of Loving God* (Shippensburg, PA: Destiny Image, 2009), 160.

61. Quoted in Roberts Liardon, *The Azuza Street Revival* (Shippensburg, PA: Destiny Image, 2006), 24.

62. Quoted in Schmitt, *Floods*, 95.

63. Quoted in Liardon, *Azuza*, 24–25.

64. Hyatt, *2000 Years*, 76.

65. DeArteaga, *Quenching*, 81.

66. Quoted in DeArteaga, *Quenching*, 84.

67. MacNutt, *Healing Reawakening*, 180.

68. DeArteaga, *Quenching*, 87.

69. Schmitt, *Floods*, 135.

70. Ibid., 137.

71. DeArteaga, *Quenching*, 90–93.

72. Schmitt, *Floods*, 101.

73. Quoted in Hyatt, *2000 Years*, 86.

74. Liardon, *Azuza*, 26.

75. Wesley, *Works*, X, 56.

76. Leigh Schmidt, *Holy Fairs*, 2d ed. (Grand Rapids, MI: Eerdmans Publishing Co., 2001), 21.

77. Ibid., 42.

78. Ibid., 145–146.

79. Quoted in DeArteaga, *Quenching*, 56.

80. Schmidt, *Fairs*, 207.

81. Wright, *Revivals*, 121.

82. Schmitt, *Floods*, 121.

83. Crowder, *Ecstasy*, 317.

84. Ibid.

85. Ibid.

86. Ibid., 317–318.

87. Ibid., 318–319.

88. Michael Talbot, *The Holographic Universe* (New York: Harper Collins, 1991), 129–131.

89. Crowder, *Ecstasy*, 321.

90. Hyatt, *2000 Years*, 95.

91. As quoted in Geoff Waugh, *Revival Fires* (Mechanicsburg, PA: Global Awakening, 2009), 27–28.

92. Schmitt, *Floods*, 125.

93. Ann Taves, *Fits, Trances, and Visions* (Princeton, NJ: Princeton University Press, 1999), 63–64.

94. John G. Arnott, *The Father's Blessing* (Lake Mary, FL: Charisma Media, 1996), 63.

CHAPTER TWO
THE METHODISTS IN ENGLAND AND AMERICA

1. Randy Clark, *There is More!* (Mechanicsburg, PA: Global Awakening, 2006), 85. Global Awakening has reprinted the original Mary Crawford book.

2. Wesley, *Works*, I, 170.

3. Schmitt, *Floods*, 128.

4. Wesley, *Works*, I, 187.

5. Ibid., 188.

6. Ibid., 189.

7. Ibid., 189–90.

8. Wesley, *Works* II, 418.

9. Ibid., 499.

10. Ibid.

11. Ibid., 506–507.

12. Wesley, *Works*, III, 106.

13. Wesley, *Works*, IV, 288.

14. Wesley, *Works*, I, 271.

15. Wesley, *Works*, IX, 27.

16. Wesley, *Works*, VIII, *Principles of a Methodist Farther Explained*,

465.

17. Wesley, *Works*, II, 204.

18. Wesley, *Works*, VII, *Sermon 89: The More Excellent Way*, 26–27.

19. Laurence Wood, *The Meaning of Pentecost in Early Methodism* (Lanham, MD: Scarecrow Press, 2002), 195.

20. Wesley, "Letter to the Rev. Dr. Middleton," 56.

21. Quoted in Eddie Hyatt, *2000 Years,* 104.

22. Wesley, *Works*, VI, 322.

23. Quoted in Vinson Synan, *The Century of the Holy Spirit* (Nashville: Thomas Nelson, 2001), 25–26.

24. John Wigger, *Taking Heaven by Storm* (Urbana, IL: University of Illinois Press, 1998), 185.

25. John Cennick, "An Account of the Most Remarkable Occurrences in the Awakenings at Bristol and Kingswood," *The Moravian Messenger,* vol. 16, cited in Arnold A. Dallimore, *George Whitefield*, vol. 1, (London: The Banner of Truth Trust, 1970), 326.

26. Wood, *Pentecost,* 191.

27. Wesley, *Works,* II, 519.

28. Wesley, *Works,* I, 204.

29. Ibid., 195–196.

30. Quoted in Arnold Lunn, *John Wesley* (New York: The Dial Press, 1929), 138.

31. Wesley, *Works,* I, 210.

32. Crowder, *Ecstasy,* 164.

33. Ibid., 165.

34. Ibid., 267.

35. Crowder, *New Mystics,* 89.

36. Wesley, *Works,* II, 510.

37. Taves, *Fits,* 57.

38. Ibid., 74.

39. Wigger, *Heaven,* 110, 123.

40. Crowder, *Ecstasy,* 282.

41. John White, *When the Spirit Comes with Power* (Downers Grove, IL: InterVarsity Press, 1988), 71.

42. Schmitt, *Floods,* 133–134.

43. Crowder, *Ecstasy,* 284.

44. Quoted in DeArteaga, *Quenching,* 28.

45. As quoted by Dallimore, *Whitefield,* vol. 2, 125.

46. Crowder, *Ecstasy,* 284–285.

47. Ibid., 285.

48. DeArteaga, *Quenching,* 41.

49. Francis MacNutt, *Overcome by the Spirit* (Grand Rapids: Chosen Books, 1990), 107.

50. Taves, *Fits,* 105.

51. Wigger, *Heaven,* 115.

52. Ibid., 112.

53. John Wigger, "Holy, 'Knock-'Em-Down' Preachers," *Christian History* 45, vol. 14, no. 1, 24.

54. MacNutt, *Overcome*, 112.

55. Wigger, *Heaven*, 114.

56. Wood, *Pentecost*, 196.

57. Crowder, *Ecstasy*, 286.

58. Quoted by Scott Kisker, "Martin Boehm, Philip William Otterbein, and the United Brethren in Christ" in *Methodist and Pietist*, J. Steven O'Malley and Jason E. Vickers, eds., (Nashville: Kingswood Books, 2011), 29–30.

59. Wigger, *Heaven*, 117.

60. Lester Ruth, *Early Methodist Life and Spirituality* (Nashville: Kingswood Books, 2005), 194–195.

61. Kenneth E. Rowe, "Jacob Albright and the Evangelical Association," in *Methodist and Pietist*, J. Steven O'Malley & Jason E. Vickers, eds., (Nashville: Kingswood Books, 2011), p. 38–39.

62. J. Steven O'Malley, "The Theological Heritage of Pietism," in *Methodist and Pietist*, 67–68.

63. William Naumann, "Doctrine and Theology in the Evangelical Association," in *Methodist and Pietist*, 94.

64. Jason E. Vickers, "The Confession of Faith: A Theological Commentary," in *Methodist and Pietist*, 128.

65. Ibid., 134–135.

66. Wigger, *Heaven*, 108.

67. Ibid., 115.

68. Ibid., 109.

69. Ibid., 117.

70. Ruth, *Early*, 195.

71. Ibid., 171.

72. Crowder, *Ecstasy*, 286.

73. Wigger, *Heaven*, 120–123.

74. Ibid., 108.

75. Ibid., 110.

76. Taves, *Fits*, 86.

77. Ruth, *Early*, 161.

78. Vinson Synan, *The Holiness-Pentecostal Movement in the United States* (Grand Rapids: Eerdmans Publishing Company, 1971), 21–22.

79. Wood, *Pentecost*. 300.

80. Synan, *Holiness*, 22.

81. Ruth, *Early*, 165–166.

82. Wesley, *Works*, I, 364.

83. Wesley, *Works*, IV, 139.

84. Ibid., 311.

85. David Lloyd, in a letter to Adam Clarke, November 7, 1821, quoted in Wood, *Pentecost*, 5.

86. Wigger, *Heaven,* 120–123.

87. Ibid., 108.

88. Ruth, *Early,* 185.

89. Richard M. Riss, *A Survey of Twentieth-Century Revival Movements in North America* (Peabody, MA: Hendrickson Publishers, 1988), 17–18.

90. Solomon B. Shaw, *Touching Incidents and Remarkable Answers to Prayer* (General Books Publication, 2009), 39. Originally published by J. W. Hazleton in 1893.

91. Robert Webster, "'Those Distracting Terrors of the Enemy': Demonic Possession and Exorcism in the Thought of John Wesley," in *The Bulletin of the John Rylands University Library of Manchester,* vol. 85, nos. 2 and 3, 380.

92. Ibid., 377.

93. Wesley, *Works,* VII, 361–370.

94. Ibid., 370–380.

95. Wesley, *Works,* I, 165.

96. Ibid., 190–191.

97. Ibid., 196–197.

98. Ibid., 234–238.

99. Ibid., 384–385.

100. Ibid., 290–291.

101. Ibid., 468.

102. Wesley, *Works,* II, 264.

103. Luke Tylerman, *The Oxford Methodists: Memoirs of the Rev. Messrs. Clayton, Ingham, Gambold, Hervey, and Broughton, with biographical notices of others.* (New York: Harper & Brothers, 1873) 131–132.

104. Quoted in Randy Clark, *Evangelism Unleashed* (Mechanicsburg, PA: Global Awakening, 2005), 39.

105. Ibid.

106. Ruth, *Early,* 177.

107. Wigger, *Heaven,* 106.

108. Ibid., 107.

109. Taves, *Fits,* 92.

110. Ibid., 93.

111. Paul Wesley Chilcote, *Her Own Story: Autobiographical Portraits of Early Methodist Women* (Nashville: Kingswood Books, 2001), 132.

112. Taves, *Fits,* 85.

113. Ibid., 109.

114. Shaw, *Touching,* 44–45.

115. Ibid., 86–87.

116. Taves, *Fits,* 241.

117. Ibid., 416.

118. Ruth, *Early,* 194.

119. Lester Ruth, *A Little Heaven Below* (Nashville: Kingswood Books, 2000), 78.

120. Ibid., 81.

121. Taves, *Fits,* 87.

122. Wigger, *Heaven,* 85–86.

123. Taves, *Fits,* 88.

124. Ibid., 90.

125. Quoted in Ruth, *Early,* 205.

126. Ruth, *Little,*189.

127. Ibid., 111.

128. Ibid., 117.

129. W. H. Daniels, *The Illustrated History of Methodism in Great Britain and America, From the Days of the Wesleys to the Present Time* (New York: Phillips & Hunt, 1880), 526.

130. Ruth, *Little,* 138–139.

131. MacNutt, *Overcome,* 107.

132. Ibid., 109.

133. Synan, *Holiness,* 24.

134. Quoted in Crowder, *Ecstasy,* 288.

135. Charles W. Ferguson, *Organizing to Beat the Devil: Methodists and the Making of America* (Garden City, NY: Doubleday & Co., 1971), 134.

136. Ibid., 135.

137. Schmidt, *Fairs,* xxv.

138. Ferguson, *Organizing,* 131–132.

139. Crowder, *Ecstasy,* 291.

140. Synan, *The Twentieth-Century Pentecostal Explosion* (Altamonte Springs, FL: Creation House, 1987), 179.

141. Hyatt, *2000 Years,* 114.

142. Mark Galli, "Revival at Cane Ridge," *Christian History* 45, vol. 14, no.1, 12.

143. Hyatt, *2000 Years,* 115.

144. Quoted in Randy Clark, *More,* 82.

145. Hyatt, *2000 Years,* 117.

146. Ferguson, *Organizing,* 142.

147. Quoted in Taves, Fits, 109–110.

148. Ferguson, *Organizing,* 128.

149. Schmitt, *Floods,* 156.

150. Quoted in Synan, *Explosion,* 25.

151. Taves, *Fits,* 105.

152. Ibid., 107–108.

153. Wigger, *Heaven,* p. 97.

154. Riss, *Twentieth Century,* 14.

155. Quoted in Randy Clark, *More,* 83.

156. James Porter, *Compendium of Methodism,* 11th ed. (Boston: George C. Rand, 1856), 474.

157. Ibid., 477.

158. Ibid., 478.

159. Riss, *Twentieth Century,* 20–21.

160. Ibid., 21.

161. Taves, *Fits,* 239.

162. DeArteaga, *Quenching,* 130.

163. Ibid.

164. Taves, *Fits,* 227–228.

165. DeArteaga, *Quenching,* 132.

166. Ibid., 134.

167. Wood, *Pentecost,* 332.

168. Ibid.

169. Riley Case, "Cutting Out Options for Seminary Education," in *We Confess* (March/April 2007), 1.

170. Taves, *Fits,* 309.

171. Ibid., 334.

172. Ibid., 346.

173. Ruth, *Early,* 165.

174. Taves, *Fits,* 77.

175. Porter, *Compendium,* 172.

176. Ibid., 173.

177. Ibid., 174.

178. Ibid., 175.

179. Schmitt, *Floods,* 156.

180. Synan, *Holiness,* 145–146.

181. Quoted in Schmitt, *Floods,* 160–161.

182. Quoted in Randy Clark, *More,* 95.

Chapter Three
Manifestations of the Spirit Among Methodist Missionaries, Central Conferences, and Autonomous Methodist Churches

1. Ramsay MacMullen, *Christianizing the Roman Empire (A.D. 100–400)* (New Haven, CT: Yale University Press, 1984), 62.

2. Craig S. Keener, *Miracles: The Credibility of the New Testament Accounts* (Grand Rapids, MI: Baker Academic, 2001), 215–216.

3. Ibid., 226.

4. Quoted in Schmitt, *Floods,* 143–144.

5. Gary McGee, "To the Regions Beyond: The Global Expansion of Pentecostalism," in Vinson Synan, ed., *The Century of the Holy Spirit* (Nashville: Thomas Nelson, 2001), 84.

6. Shaw, *Touching Incidents,* 160–161.

7. As quoted in Luther Oconer, *Methodism in Asia and the Pacific,* T & T Clark Companion to Methodism, Charles Yrigoyen Jr., ed. (New York: T & T Clark International, 2010), 163.

8. As quoted in Brenton T. Badley, *Warne of India: The Life-Story of Bishop Francis Wesley Warne* (Madras, India: Madras Publishing House, 1932), 17.

9. Quoted in Geoff Waugh, *Revival Fires,* 96.

10. Quoted in Synan, *The Century,* 92.

11. Quoted in Hyatt, *2000 Years,* 159.

12. Ibid., 7.

13. Quoted in Randy Clark, *Supernatural Missions* (Mechanicsburg, PA: Global Awakening, 2012), 34.

14. Riss, *Twentieth Century,* 65–66.

15. Wright, *Revivals,* 174.

16. Schmitt, *Floods,* 192.

17. Synan, *Century,* 302.

18. Ibid., 314.

19. Quoted in Luther Oconer, *Methodism,* 163.

20. Synan, *Century,* 88.

21. Clark, *Supernatural Missions,* 24–25.

22. Hwa Yung, "A 21st-Century Reformation: Recover the Supernatural," *Christianity Today,* September 11, 2010.

23. Luther J. Oconer, *The Culto Pentecostal Story: Holiness Revivalism and the Making of Philippine Methodist Identity, 1899-1965,* PhD Dissertation, Drew University, 2009, 94–95.

24. Ibid., 23.

25. Ibid., 178–179.

26. Ibid., 187–190.

27. Ibid., 3–4.

28. *Mission Society News,* August 25, 2011, "The Lady from Baga."

29. Quoted in Luther Oconer, *Methodism,* 162.

30. Larry Davies, www.sowingseedsoffaith.com, accessed February 26, 2012.

31. As quoted in Randy Clark, *Evangelism Unleashed,* 68.

32. *Mission Society News,* September 2012, "Should We Expect a Miracle?" This issue of the newsletter has a number of healing stories from various mission fields.

33. Ibid., "God Knows Our Needs: Unborn Baby Is Healed."

Chapter Four
Twentieth- and Twenty-First-Century Manifestations of the Spirit Among Methodists

1. Roberts Liardon, *Azuza Street,* 65–66.

2. Schmitt, *Floods,* 182.

3. Liardon, *Azuza Street,* 90.

4. Riss, *Twentieth Century,* 31.

5. Ibid., 43.

6. Ibid., 44–45.

7. Ibid., 49–50.

8. Quoted in Riss, *Twentieth Century,* 50.

9. Ibid.

10. Quoted in Taves, *Fits,* 333.

11. Quoted in Riss, *Twentieth Century,* 81.

12. Taves, *Fits,* 337, emphasis added.

13. See Roberts Liardon, *God's Generals: Why They Succeeded and Why Some Failed* (New Kensington, PA: Whitaker House, 1996).

14. James and Molly Scott, *Restoring Methodism: Ten Decisions for United Methodist Churches in America* (Dallas: Provident Publishing, 2006), 127–128.

15. Wright, *Revivals*, 218.

16. Thomas Bandy, *Circuit Rider*, September-Octobert 2007, Vol. 31, No. 5, 28.

17. The article "Are There Children on Your Healing Rooms Team?" appeared in the August/September 2011 issue of the International Association of Healing Rooms newsletter.

18. James Wagner, *Blessed to Be a Blessing* (Nashville, Upper Room Books, 1980).

19. James Wagner, *An Adventure in Healing and Wholeness: The Healing Ministry of Christ in the Church Today,* (Nashville: Upper Room Books, 1993).

CHAPTER FIVE
WHY ARE SIGNS AND WONDERS IMPORTANT?

1. MacNutt, *Reawakening*, 50–51.

2. Bill Johnson, *Release the Power of Jesus* (Shippensburg, PA: Destiny Image, 2009), 168.

3. John Cennick, "An Account of the Most Remarkable Occurrences in the Awakenings at Bristol and Kingswood," *The Moravian Messenger,* Vol. 16; cited in Arnold A. Dallimore, *George Whitefield*, vol. 1, 326.

4. Wesley, *Works*, II, 519.

5. Ibid.

6. Ibid.

7. Johnson, *Release*, 26.

8. Ibid., 119.

9. Ibid., 140.

10. Terry Teykl, *Making Room to Pray: How to Start and Maintain a Prayer Room in Your Church* (Muncie, IN: Prayer Point Press, 1993).

11. Johnson, *Release*, 122.

12. Ibid., 77.

13. Ibid., 143.

14. Ibid., 145.

15. Ibid., 152.

16. George Santayana, 1905–1906, *Reason in Common Sense,* vol. 1, chap. 12.

APPENDIX 3
A CYCLONE OF POWER AND GLORY IN ANSWER TO PRAYER

1. Solomon B. Shaw, in *Touching Incidents and Remarkable Answers to Prayer* (Lansing, MI: J. W. Hazleton, 1893), 107–108.

ABOUT
ALDERSGATE RENEWAL MINISTRIES

THE MISSION OF Aldersgate Renewal Ministries (ARM) is to equip the local church to minister to the world in the power of the Holy Spirit. ARM serves the local church by providing dynamic learning experiences that educate participants to live in the power of the Holy Spirit.

In Matthew 28:18–20, and in 10:6–8, Jesus commands us to "go." But Jesus also makes it clear that the grace to proclaim and to demonstrate the gospel to the ends of the earth comes from the power of the Holy Spirit (Acts 1:8). The Holy Spirit's power is essential in carrying on the ministry of Jesus!

ARM seeks to build a long-term, mutual ministry relationship to help the church keep in step with the leading of the Holy Spirit. As the local church learns to walk in the Spirit, to pray and to worship in the Spirit, and to share its faith empowered by the Spirit, the Great Commission is fulfilled in the character and power of Jesus Christ.

Established in 1978, ARM functions as a 501(c)(3) nonprofit corporation. ARM is sustained by the grace of God through the gifts of individuals and churches who have caught the vision of equipping every local church to minister to the world in the power of the Holy Spirit.

ARM ministries span the world locally, nationally, and internationally. We invite you to become involved in what God is doing through Aldersgate Renewal Ministries.

ARM recognizes the biblical standard for good stewardship and adheres to the policies of the Evangelical Council for Financial Accountability.

Website: www.aldersgaterenewal.org
E-mail: info@aldersgaterenewal.org

ABOUT THE AUTHOR

FRANK H. BILLMAN graduated from Houghton College, Houghton, New York, magna cum laude in 1975 with a BA in religion with minors in Christian education and psychology. He was ordained a deacon in the United Methodist Church in 1976. He graduated from Trinity Evangelical Divinity School, Deerfield, Illinois, cum laude with a Master of Divinity degree from the School of Christian Education in 1978. He graduated from Trinity Evangelical Divinity School in 1979 with a Master of Theology degree in pastoral counseling and psychology. He was ordained an elder in the United Methodist Church in 1980. He graduated from Eastern Baptist Theological Seminary (now Palmer Theological Seminary), St. David's, Pennsylvania, in 1988 with a Doctor of Ministry degree in church growth and evangelism.

He has served as a pastor of United Methodist churches continuously since 1979. In July 2005, Frank became part-time Director of Church Relations at Aldersgate Renewal Ministries. In that role, he oversees several local church renewal programs and international and cross-cultural ministries, and he serves as Dean of the Methodist School for Supernatural Ministry.

He has been a speaker at national Aldersgate conferences, at sessions of the Methodist School for Supernatural Ministry, at local church renewal events, at revivals, and at retreats. He has led ministry teams to Tanzania, Nepal, Liberia, and a prison.

As part of his duties with Aldersgate Renewal Ministries, Frank serves as an adjunct professor in the doctoral program at United Theological Seminary in Dayton, Ohio, leading a Doctor of Ministry program in supernatural ministry, the first of its kind in the country.

He has had articles published in several publications. His previous book, published by Aldersgate Renewal Ministries, was *Shepherding Renewal.*

Frank resides with his wife, Peggi, in Joelton, Tennessee. He has three sons, Luke, Nic, and Tito.

CONTACT THE AUTHOR

Website:
www.aldersgaterenewal.org

E-mail:
info@aldersgaterenewal.org